W2 TAX PREPARATION MADE EASY

DR. R. AHMED

Copyrights and Trademarks

ISBN: 979-8-9878572-7-4

Table of Contents

DISCLAIMER

This book, the author, and Book Passion LLC does not provide tax, legal or accounting advice. This material has been prepared for informational purposes only, and is not intended to provide, and should not be relied on for, tax, legal or accounting advice. You should consult your own tax, legal and accounting advisors before engaging in any transaction.

ACKNOWLEDGMENTS

I want to thank God (for answering my prayers when most needed), my wife, Dr. Saleema, (for being a pillar of strength in times of weakness), my sons Zeeshan & Faizan (for being the 'why' in my life), my parents Nasir & Dr. Safia (for teaching me resilience) and last but not least, my readers for taking the time to not only read my material but also for providing valuable feedback, inspiration, and motivation which encourages me to become a better writer and to provide high-quality content. Thank you!

Introduction

Filing taxes can be confusing and stressful, especially if you do not know which forms to use or how to fill them out.

Fear of not knowing if you've done things correctly. You may be afraid that you owe the IRS money. The task of gathering piles is a hassle. The tax maze is a confusing place for those who work with W2. This doesn't have to be the case.

The book will guide you through the stressful path of tax preparation. The book will make the intimidating task of tax filing so easy. No more IRS correspondence or tax worries on how to prepare for your W2 tax.

The book is your friend during tax season. There is no need to hire an accountant. With the tips and tricks provided, you will be a tax expert.

Why is this book different from others? This is not a book filled with unintelligible code. The advice is presented humorously and entertainingly, so you can skip the arcane terminology and go straight to what I have for you. You can easily understand and apply everything you learn by following simple, easy steps.

You'll use these pages to prepare your taxes the most. You'll discover:

- How to read your W-2 like a pro

- Filling out each tax form correctly requires instructions.

- All tax credits and deductions are available to you.

- Red flags can trigger audits.

- How to maximize your tax refund

- Common questions about W2s answered

Don't waste time or money paying excessive taxes. This book will help you maximize your refund and prepare your taxes with no fear.

The W2 form is also known as Wage and Tax Statements. Before the end of the year, both the IRS and the employee must receive this document. W-2s report the employee's salary, bonuses, and other types of compensation. W-2s also show the taxes that were withheld at the federal, state, and municipal levels.

Any employer that pays at least 600 dollars to an employee during the calendar year must provide a W2. It doesn't matter if the employee is a family member. W-2s are required to include any earnings over $600, including non-cash payments. If Social Security and Medicare taxes have been withheld, a W-2 will be required.

What is the importance of a W-2 for employees with W2s when filing their taxes? W-2s give the IRS the income and tax information they need to verify that you paid the correct amount of taxes. W-2s already show the tax deducted already from your income, so you can decide if any more tax is owed or if you are eligible for a tax return. The W-2 contains all the necessary information to determine what you are owed.

Check your W-2 for accuracy before filing your tax return. Check that the information on your W-2 is accurate. This includes checking to make sure you have entered all of the correct details, including the employer name, Social Security number, and mailing address. Verify that your wages and the amounts deducted from them match those on your payslip. Report any errors to your employer and get a corrected W-2 before filing.

Don't waste time or money paying excessive taxes. This book will help you maximize your refund and prepare your return with no fear.

Chapter 1

Tax Planning and Long-Term Financial Goals

It's crucial to consider the big picture when managing your money. Your long-term goals should be reflected in the tax decisions that you take today, as well as how you save money, spend it, and invest it. Taxes directly affect your income and ability to build wealth.

Financial Goals

Establishing financial goals over different time periods will help you visualize how to make wise financial decisions. Short-term goals, such as saving money for a trip or paying off credit card debt, can make spending and budgeting easier. Saving for a home, a car, or bringing up a family are medium-term goals that can motivate you to make more strategic choices about investing and planning for retirement.

Keep your long-term financial goals top of mind. For example, the retirement lifestyle or legacy you wish to leave for your children will influence major decisions such as what type of account to open, how much to risk, and where to live. You can create a plan that will help you achieve long-term financial stability by incorporating all of your financial goals into the larger picture.

The correct goals help put temptations in perspective. You can make the right financial decisions now to ensure your future security, freedom, and prosperity.

A credible financial plan is essential to any journey toward your long-term financial goals. Financial planning is the process of converting your goals and dreams into financial milestones and mapping them against current and future financial resources. The basis of financial planning, then, is based on four fundamental assumptions.

1. Financial plans must generate the maximum possible return on investment for an organization.

You should be willing to accept a certain level of risk.

2. Financial planning must ensure the lowest possible risk for the target return you aim to achieve.

3. Your financial plan should include liquidity. It must also ensure you have the right amount of liquidity when needed.

4. Your financial plan should be tax-efficient. It means that you must judge your returns concerning the post-tax return.

In this book, we will only focus on the tax aspect. At different stages in your financial planning, taxation is important.

Directly and indirectly, taxes influence your financial decisions. Tax implications are important to understand if you want to optimize your finances and keep as much of your hard-earned money while meeting your legal obligations.

Tax Planning

Tax-planning is key; you need to know what taxes to pay, how flexible your plan can be, and when to make key financial decisions to maximize the benefits. Integrating tax planning with your financial plan will allow you to better manage your cash flow, make smarter investments, and keep more of the money that you have worked so hard for. (We will talk about it later in the book.)

Here are the types of taxes you pay:

Types of Taxes you pay

Taxes you may pay include state and federal income taxes.

The tax rates vary significantly from one state to another and even within a city. It's like a puzzle trying to figure out how everything fits together.

Federal Income Task

Federal income taxes are taxes you pay to help the country pay for everything from national defense to Social Security and health and safety net programs. During election time, candidates often talk about their ideas for who to tax more and who to give more tax breaks to. Even a president cannot implement any changes to the federal income tax code without Congress's support.

State Income Task

Unlike federal income taxes, states vary in the manner in which they tax their residents' income. State income taxes primarily pay for big, state-run functions such as education, health care, corrections, and transportation.

Taxes on Property

Property tax is a tax that you pay on something you own, most often your house. In all states, local governments like the county or city usually impose property taxes. State property taxes account for only 1% of the state's revenue but 50% of local revenues, which are used to fund services like public schools, road repairs, and law enforcement.

If you are considering an upgrade to your home or a purchase, this is one way that you can control your taxes. You can't pay property taxes off like a mortgage. They are due each year, and they may even increase. Property taxes are usually higher when you own a larger property.

Taxes on Payroll

You'll see that various taxes have already been deducted from your pay. These withholdings are used to cover federal income taxes, Social Security, and Medicare.

In 2023, the Social Security Tax rate will be 6.2% for earnings of up to $160,200. Medicare taxes are 1.45% of all income. There will be an equal amount of matching from both you and your employer. The self-employed pay 12.4% of Social Security tax and 2.9% of Medicare themselves.

Some states tax wages to fund disability insurance programs and leave for family members. While you may not see this on your paycheck, the employer is paying a payroll tax to pay for unemployment insurance.

Although tax rates may not be within your control, you can still use strategies to lower your tax burden. Tax planning is a great way to save money over the long term.

Contributing pre-tax money to retirement accounts like 401(k)s and traditional IRAs is usually the easiest way to reduce taxable income. You can also use flexible spending accounts to pay for dependent care or health care. Work-related deductions are another option.

Be sure to know which credits and deductions are available each year. Tax credits, for example, for energy efficiency, education, children, or charitable donations, as well as deductions on mortgage interest and business costs, can result in thousands of dollars saved annually. A tax expert can help you find reduction strategies that are tailored to your specific financial circumstances.

If you feel that your property has been undervalued, you can appeal the assessment. The cumulative savings of lowering assessments over time can be significant. Some states also have property tax exemptions or caps for seniors and other groups.

While Social Security and Medicare taxes are set, it is possible to lower your taxable income for payroll tax purposes by increasing contributions made before tax. Pre-tax dollars saved in a 401(k), traditional IRA, or other retirement plan reduce payroll taxes for the current year, as well as build up your retirement fund.

Important Aspects of Tax Planning

Tax planning is important for W-2 employees to maximize their take-home income and optimize their financial situation. Why is it important?

1. You can reduce your tax liability by understanding the income credits and deductions you have. By doing so, you will be able to make more informed choices throughout the year that could lower your tax. You can do this by contributing to retirement plans like IRAs and 401(k), maximizing your deductions such as dependent care, student loan interest or itemizing deductions if they benefit you more.

2. Plan ahead to avoid any last-minute fumbling and possible errors. Choosing the best filing method, including online, paper, or professional assistance, can help you save money by reducing the amount of late filing fees and penalties.

3. Plan for your future goals. Tax planning can help you reach your financial objectives in the long term. Understanding your tax bracket as well as how your financial choices impact your taxes will help you make better decisions about your investments, retirement plans, and savings strategies.

4. Tax benefits for W-2 employees are also available. These include the Earned Income Tax Credit for those with low and medium incomes, as well as the Dependent Care Credit for expenses related to childcare. These benefits can reduce your tax burden if you know how to use them.

5. Tax laws can be confusing. Unfamiliarity may lead you to make costly errors, like missing out on deductions or claiming credits that are not eligible. You might also file it incorrectly. Tax planning can help you avoid costly mistakes and understand your obligations.

Tax planning may seem complicated, but it does not have to be. That is why you are reading this book to learn about taxes. There are many resources available as well, including online calculators, government sites, and even consulting a professional. Plan ahead to understand your situation, and you will be able to enjoy a reduced tax bill as well as a secure financial future.

Tax Decisions That Align with Financial Goals

Tax planning is a crucial part of personal financial management. It can help individuals and their families achieve their financial objectives over varying time frames. It is important to align tax strategies with both short-term and long-term goals when making tax decisions.

Tax decisions can optimize cash flow for short-term goals such as saving up money for a down payment on a home or building an emergency reserve. Tax strategies like increasing 401(k), lowering taxable income, or using tax credits and deductions can help people save more money year after year. This extra money can be used to save and spend in the near future. Tax-advantaged accounts such as IRAs and 401(k)s also allow people to invest funds that would otherwise be used for taxes and enjoy tax-deferred gains over time.

Over a longer period of time, advanced tax planning is used to support objectives such as retirement planning, legacy and estate plans, business investments, etc. Retirement accounts will transition from being purely savings vehicles into sources of retirement income. At this point, managing the required minimum distributions and withdrawing in sequence is key to avoiding being pushed unnecessarily into higher tax brackets. Establishing trusts and gifting assets to heirs can reduce future estate tax to pass wealth on to them. In business, decisions about entity structuring, dividends versus owner's draws, and other tax options support profitability and long-term growth.

People often consider moving to a more tax-friendly state later in life as part of their retirement planning. States like Florida and Texas, which do not tax pensions or retirement account withdrawals, allow people to save more in retirement. It is worth planning for these moves in an overall financial plan because of the substantial tax savings that can be realized over decades of retirement.

A growing number of people are living longer and accumulating more healthcare costs. This requires tax-optimized planning. Health savings accounts provide triple tax benefits by allowing for tax-deductible contributions today, tax-free growth, and tax-free withdrawals in the future for qualified medical expenses. Early HSA use, even in the working years, will give you more time to accumulate funds. These accounts can then be used to offset medical bills and Medicare premiums in retirement.

Businesses of all sizes, large and small, use tax mitigation for both short-term and long-term time frames. Cash flow management is similar to personal finances. Tax payments and refunds from year to year are important. Strategic decisions on growth initiatives like investing in R&D or new equipment provide large tax credits and deductions that reduce tax exposure while aiming to boost profit over time.

Advanced Tax Planning Strategies

People with complicated financial situations can use these strategies because they are more advanced than the fundamentals. To ensure that these strategies comply with the tax laws, they require professional advice and careful consideration.

Strategies for Business

Tax planning for businesses includes:

- **Entity selection and incorporation**:

Choosing a business structure such as an LLC or a corporation can have important tax implications. Taxation, liability protection, and operational flexibility are all factors that affect the advantages and disadvantages of each entity type.

- **Using Business Expense Deductions**: It is important to properly identify and maximize eligible business expenses in order to reduce taxable income. To implement advanced strategies, it is necessary to carefully review expenses for them to meet the tax code requirements.

- **Hiring Family Members**: Hiring family members may provide tax benefits, particularly if they are contributing to the legitimate operation of your business. Employing family members can allow you to shift your income into lower tax brackets. You will also be able to provide income for them while minimizing payroll taxes and making contributions to their retirement account.

Estate planning and gifting

Tax planning opportunities arise from estate planning and gifts.

- **Understanding Estate and Gift Tax Rules:** Estate planning involves strategic asset management and wealth transfers to minimize estate taxes at death. Wills, trusts, and other legal tools are used to efficiently distribute assets. Knowing the estate tax exclusions and exemptions and how to plan can reduce taxes on assets transferred to beneficiaries.

- **Use Lifetime Gift Exemptions:** Individuals can make gifts tax-free up to certain limits, both annually and over a lifetime. These exemptions allow you to transfer assets during your lifetime, which reduces your estate tax.

- **Trusts to Reduce Taxes:** Irrevocable trusts such as charitable remainder trusts or grantor retained annuity (GRAT) trusts allow you to transfer assets while still retaining control.

Donations

Donating to charities to help those who are in need is an effective tax-planning strategy. Take into consideration the following:

- Donations to charities can be tax-deductible. Charitable donations made to organizations that qualify may provide tax advantages. Donating cash, appreciated property, or assets may qualify you for tax deductions.

- Think about donor-advised funds: These funds allow you to donate to charity and get a tax deduction immediately, while also recommending specific charities to receive grants over time.

- Evaluating Charitable Restraint Trusts: Charitable restraint trusts offer a way to give back while maintaining a steady income. Transferring assets to a charitable remainder trust (CRT) can provide you with a tax deduction for the current year, reduce your capital gains tax, and allow you to receive income over a certain period.

How to File Taxes

To ensure that you are complying with the tax laws and reporting your financial data accurately, there are several steps involved in filing taxes.

1. Determining Your Business Structure

Determine the type of legal structure your business has, whether it is a corporation, LLC, or sole proprietorship. The legal structure of your small business determines the tax forms that you must submit.

2. Obtain an employer identification number (EIN).

Apply for your EIN with the IRS if you have not already. The IRS requires this unique number for tax purposes.

3. Maintain accurate financial records.

Keep accurate records of your company's expenses, income, and receipts. Also, keep bank statements, invoices, bills, bank statements, etc. You can use this information to accurately calculate your income tax and make deductions.

4. Select an accounting method.

Choose between cash and accrual accounting to track the income and expenditures of your business. The accounting method that you select determines the timing of when revenue is recognized and expenses are deducted.

5. Calculate your tax year.

Choose whether you want to run your business on a 12-month calendar (from January 1 to December 31) or an annual fiscal period (any 12-month consecutive period). The majority of small businesses operate in a calendar year.

6. Understanding Your Tax Obligations

Be familiar with your specific business tax obligations. Included in this are income taxes, taxes on self-employment, and employment taxes.

The Tax Filing Process: Common Myths

Taxes are an annual event that can cause a lot of different types of anxiety. The mention of tax forms, deductions, or the approaching deadline can cause shivers to run down the spine and create stomach knots. Fear not, tired taxpayers! It is important to dispel some common misconceptions about tax preparation before diving into an ocean of W-2s. We can then embark on a journey that is surprisingly effortless and even enjoyable.

Myths #1: Taxes are complicated. "I'm going to mess up."

Reality: Although the tax code can sometimes seem like a confusing alphabetic soup, it isn't as complicated as you think. When navigating simple tax returns, web-based tools and software that are easy to use are often used. Remember that you're not the only one. If you are feeling overwhelmed, this book is a great resource. You will learn more by the end of the book.

Myth #2: "I'm self-employed/freelance, so my taxes are a nightmare."

Reality: Self-employment is not synonymous with tax confusion. It's important to keep accurate and organized records. Keep detailed records of all your expenses and income. Also, learn about the various deductions that are available for self-employed people. Amazingly, how easy (and useful!) filing can be. You may not realize how simple (and useful!) filing can be.

Myth #3: "I always have to pay money for taxes." "I hate paying more taxes than I do already!"

Reality: Not everyone is owed! Many taxpayers are eligible for refunds. Make sure you are taking advantage of your deductions and credit throughout the entire year. You may be pleasantly surprised by the results.

Myth #4: "It doesn't matter if you submit your tax return late." Will they remember in a few days?

Reality: False. The consequences of filing late can vary, depending on the circumstances. However, late filing will result in interest and fines that could quickly diminish any refund. Do your taxes on time, or even earlier! Avoid stress and financial strain.

Myth #5 Taxes are boring. " Who cares?

Reality: Taxes can provide an interesting insight into the economic and social trends of a society. You can engage in important conversations about government spending and resource allocation by understanding the tax system. Even the tax-averse can benefit from claiming your legal credits and deductions.

Myth #6: "The IRS wants me." Audits are open to everyone!

Reality: Audits are rarer than people think. The IRS gives priority to sophisticated taxpayers who have filed red flags. If you are honest and maintain good records, the chances of being audited are slim.

Myth #7: "Filing electronically is risky." "Someone is going to steal my identity!"

Online filing is safer than paper filing. E-filing is a safe option because it has strong security measures. Use caution when selecting a reliable site, and avoid dubious links.

Myth #8: "I'm not rich enough to pay taxes."

Reality: Low-income taxpayers can qualify for significant tax deductions and credits that could lower their tax liabilities or result in a tax refund. It is worth investigating your options, regardless of your financial status.

Myth #9: "Hiring an accountant is prohibitively costly." I can do it myself.

Reality: It is possible to do your taxes yourself, but a professional tax preparer can save you money and time. They will be able to spot any potential credits and deductions, ensure accuracy, and deal with any problems that might arise. You should weigh the cost of hiring them against the value they can bring.

Myth #10: Taxes are unfair. "The wealthy can pay less tax."

Reality: The tax system may be complex, but the basic structure is progressive. This means that people with more income pay a higher percentage of taxes. Wealth and income are also taxed in different ways, so many rich people must pay substantial taxes on capital gains.

Chapter 2

Understanding Taxable and Non-Taxable Income

In Chapter 1, we looked at the role that taxation plays in helping families and individuals achieve their financial goals. In this chapter, we'll discuss the difference between taxable and untaxable income. The Internal Revenue Service (IRS), which is the federal tax authority, distinguishes between these two categories of income. Federal income taxes won't apply to all of the money a person or household receives.

This chapter will give an overview of taxable income. It includes regular income, such as salaries and wages, as well as irregular earnings, like prizes and gifts. We will also explain which sources of income are not subject to federal taxation. Understanding what income is taxed and what is not will help you and your family better plan for the future. Taxpayers can calculate their tax liability more accurately if they understand the difference between taxable income and non-taxable income.

What is taxable income?

The term taxable income is used for the compensation of individuals or businesses that is used to calculate tax liabilities. Gross income or total income amounts are used to determine how much an individual or business owes for a specific tax period.

Taxable Income Includes all forms of compensation in cash, services, and property. Unless specifically exempted from taxation by law, all income is taxable. It should be included in your income tax return.

What are the different types of taxable income?

Failure to report income taxes can have serious consequences. To be certain that you pay taxes on all types of income, we've listed them below.

1. **Compensation and Benefits for Employees**

Wages and salaries, as well as fringe benefits, are among the most common types of income that is taxable.

2. **Income from investments and businesses**

Self-employed people are subject to taxes, specifically through the income of their businesses. Net rental income, for example, and partnership income are taxable.

3. **Earnings from self-employment or the gig economy**

IRS taxes income earned through contract, freelance, or gig work. The IRS considers income earned from ride-sharing apps, rental properties on short-term rental marketplaces, and other forms of self-employment.

- Interest Income

The interest earned on assets such as savings and checking accounts, bonds, bills, mortgages, and other loans is considered taxable income. Interest, no matter how small the amount, must be declared.

- Dividends:

Dividends received on stock, mutual funds, and other assets are taxed. All dividends must also be declared, just like interest.

4. Scholarships, grants, and fellowships that are tax-deductible

Taxable income can include some tuition costs and related expenses, depending on the degree candidate.

5. Rent:

The income from renting out property becomes taxable after deducting expenses like mortgage interest, maintenance costs, and depreciation.

6. Capital Gains:

A capital gains tax is imposed on any profits from selling investment assets such as stocks, bonds, and precious metals. Capital gains are taxed differently for short-term and long-term capital gains.

Non-taxable income:

The other is income received that does not have to be taxed. Even if these forms of compensation are not taxed, they must still be included in your tax return. Non-taxable income includes:

1. **The Gifts of Inheritance**

The most common tax situations that are misunderstood involve gifts and inheritances. IRS guidelines state that inheritances and gifts are excluded from taxable income. If you get $10,000 as a gift from your aunt or $50,000 from your grandmother who passed away, then you don't have to pay any income tax on these funds.

There are a few exceptions, though. In some instances, income from assets that are gifted or inherited can be taxed. If you inherit rental property, for example, all rental income must be declared. The rules for inherited retirement accounts, such as 401(k), IRAs, and other similar plans, have also been changed to require withdrawals at a certain age. These withdrawals are reported on your tax return. The original inheritance, i.e., the dollar amount that was left behind to heirs, is tax-free.

A less common situation where inheritances are taxable is when objects have significantly increased in value over the years compared with their initial purchase price. Even if an item was bought for $1,000 and is worth $50,000 today, it may be necessary to calculate the capital gains of $49,000 in order to report taxes on the inheritance.

2. Winning the lottery and Sweepstakes

We all have a dream of winning millions of dollars in a lottery or sweepstakes. While that windfall of cash may seem like an incredible stroke of good luck, there are tax implications. Even if the winnings are received in a lump sum, they must still be declared to the IRS. The sponsoring organization uses a W-2G to report your winnings. The tax rate is calculated based on the federal income tax bracket that you are in. State tax authorities may also claim a share of the gaming winnings that are paid out to their residents.

Annuities are a smarter financial strategy than a lump-sum payout for large lottery winners or sweepstakes prizewinners. Since the annual payments are considered income, they will be taxed as soon as you get them, not all at once. It prevents you from being pushed into the highest tax bracket the moment you receive your winnings and having to pay a large tax bill at one time. It does, however, require careful budgeting and management of the funds for decades before the entire amount is paid under the annuity.

3. Cancelling Debt

Under certain circumstances, canceled debts can be a pleasant surprise. Normal, cancelled debts, such as credit card principals reduced through short sales or loan modifications, are taxable. Mortgage debt relief can be exempt from taxation if it occurs in the years immediately following the end of the 2000s housing crisis under federal programs. This tax credit is available to homeowners who have experienced foreclosures or are struggling with underwater home loans.

You should investigate if you are eligible for an exemption that will allow you to deduct the amount of canceled debt from your total taxable income for the year. If you fail to apply for an exemption, even if it is legitimately available, then the income could be declared tax-free.

4. The Return of Damaged Goods and Refunds

The majority of everyday product refunds reverse the purchase, and there is no impact on taxes. Sometimes retailers will refund the money for goods returned that are damaged, missing, or unusable in any other way. Technically, even expired food items returned to a retailer for refund fall into this category. In some cases, the IRS could consider compensation that goes beyond simply negating an original purchase as "gain" in some cases. For tax purposes, it may be classified as taxable miscellaneous income, on top of regular income and wages.

According to the IRS definition of "de minimis benefits," taxpayers can claim up to 600 dollars. These are minor refunds for damaged items (e.g., a 10-dollar refund on cheese that has gone moldy). If you don't regularly receive refunds for items that exceed $600 per year, then you probably do not have to include these amounts in your tax return. Double-check all your records, and consult a professional tax advisor if you are unsure.

5. Jury duty payment

Sometimes civic responsibilities are more than just a moral duty. They can also benefit the taxpayer. Jury duty usually comes with a daily allowance to cover travel expenses, such as transportation and food. Jurors can also receive compensation for trials lasting weeks or even months. The compensation may not be a lot, but it is still taxable and must be reported.

Calculating Taxable Income

Each year, workers are required to calculate their tax to be paid. Some people are able to do this by themselves using the taxable income formula.

What is the taxable income formula?

Calculate the total tax due under income tax using the taxable income formula. The formula for calculating taxable income is simple. Calculated by subtracting all the deductions and exemptions allowed under income tax laws from total earnings. Businesses calculate it by subtracting the costs and deductibles from their total income and revenue.

It is the income that an individual or organization earns, which may result in a tax obligation. It is very easy to calculate the taxable income of an individual. To do this, subtract all expenses that are exempt from tax and any applicable deductions.

It is written as:

Formula for Taxable Income: Total Gross Income minus Total Excise + Total Deductions

The calculation of the taxable income of a company is made by subtracting **the cost of the goods sold** from its gross sales, **the operating expenses**, and the interest on the debts. To arrive at the final income, a deduction or credit for tax is also adjusted.

It is written as:

Formula for Taxable Income = Gross Sales + Cost of Goods Sold + Operating Expenses + Interest Expenses + Tax Credit/Deduction.

Explanation

Four steps can be used to calculate the taxable income of an individual:

1. Determine the gross total income for the person. The gross total income is the sum of all income sources, such

as salary and wages, rent from a property, gains on asset sales, and incomes from business.

2. Then, calculate the total number of exemptions that the person has received. Among the different types of exemptions are charitable donations, humanitarian aid, education materials, and so on. Lists may differ depending on which country you are reporting from.

3. Then, calculate the total number of deductions that apply to an individual's earnings. Tax deductions can include student loans, home loan interest, medical costs, etc. The list can also differ depending on where you are filing.

4. The formula for calculating taxable earnings is to subtract the total of the exemptions or deductions made from gross total income.

Four steps can be used to calculate the taxable income of an organization:

Step 1. First, the gross sales must be verified by your sales department.

Step 2: The cost of the goods is calculated by the accounting department.

Step 3: Next, you will need to calculate the cost of operating expenses.

Step 4: The interest is then calculated using the outstanding debt of the business and the current interest rate.

Rate of Interest * Debt = Interest Expense

Step 5: Calculate all tax credits and deductions applicable to your company.

Step 6: Subtracting the costs of goods sold and the interest on debts from the company's gross sales completes the calculation of taxable income.

Taxable Income = Gross Sales - Cost of Goods Sold - Operating Expense - Interest Expense - Tax Deduction/Credit

Example 1:

Take Jay as an example in order to better understand how the tax is calculated. His son has a $30,000 education loan, and he pays interest on it at 6%. A tax exemption worth $10,000 is available to him.

Below is the data for the calculation of David's taxable earnings.

	A	B
1	Gross Salary	$70,000
2	Education Loan	$30,000
3	Interest on Education Loan	10%
4	Tax Exemption	$10,000

Therefore, Jay's Taxable Income can be calculated as,

	A	B
1	Gross Salary	$70,000
2	Education Loan	$30,000
3	Interest on Education Loan	10%
4	Tax Exemption	$10,000
5	Taxable Income	=B1-B3*B2-B4

Taxable Earning = Gross salary − Interest on education loan −
Tax exemptions
= $70,000 − 10% * $30,000 − $10,000
= $57,000

	A	B
1	Gross Salary	$70,000
2	Education Loan	$30,000
3	Interest on Education Loan	10%
4	Tax Exemption	$10,000
5	Taxable Income	$57,000

Therefore, Jay's taxable Earning is **$57,000.**
Example 2
Take this example of Apple Inc.'s annual report from 2020, 2021
and 2022. This table shows a summary of the detailed
calculations of taxable incomes for 2020, 2021 and 2022. You
can find the following information:
The table below shows data for the calculation of taxable
earnings of Apple Inc.'s annual report for the years 2020, 2021,
and 2022

	A	B	C	D
1		**Years End in Millions**		
2	Particulars	**June 29, 2020**	**June 30, 2021**	**June 25, 2022**
3	Net Sales	$265,595	$224,234	$215,639
4	Cost of Sales	$163,756	$141,048	$131,376
5	Research and Development	$14,236	$11,581	$10,045
6	Selling, General and administrative	$16,705	$15,261	$14,194
7	Non-Operating Income	$5,245	$5,068	$2,804
8	Interest Expenses	$3,240	$2,323	$1,456

The taxable Income of Apple Inc.'s annual report for the year 2016 can be calculated as,

	A	B	C	D
1		**Years End in Millions**		
2	Particulars	**June 29, 2020**	**June 30, 2021**	**June 25, 2022**
3	Net Sales	$265,595	$224,234	$215,639
4	Cost of Sales	$163,756	$141,048	$131,376
5	Research and Development	$14,236	$11,581	$10,045
6	Selling, General and administrative	$16,705	$15,261	$14,194
7	Non-Operating Income	$5,245	$5,068	$2,804
8	Interest Expenses	$3,240	$2,323	$1,456
9	Taxable Income			=D3-D4-D5-D6+D7-D8

Taxable Earning= Net sales – Research and development expense – Selling, general and administrative expense – Interest expense + Non-operating income

= $215,639 – $131,376 – $10,045 – $14,194 – $1,456 + $2,804

Taxable Earnings = $61,372

	A	B	C	D
1		**Years End in Millions**		
2	Particulars	**June 29, 2020**	**June 30, 2021**	**June 25, 2022**
3	Net Sales	$265,595	$224,234	$215,639

4	Cost of Sales	$163,756	$141,048	$131,376
5	Research and Development	$14,236	$11,581	$10,045
6	Selling, General and administrative	$16,705	$15,261	$14,194
7	Non-Operating Income	$5,245	$5,068	$2,804
8	Interest Expenses	$3,240	$2,323	$1,456
9	Taxable Income			$61,372

Therefore, the taxable earnings of Apple Inc. stood at **$61,372** Mn for the year 2022.

The Taxable Earning of Apple Inc.'s annual report for the year 2021 and 2021 can be calculated as,

	A	B	C	D
1		**Years End in Millions**		
2	Particulars	**June 29, 2020**	**June 30, 2021**	**June 25, 2022**
3	Net Sales	$265,595	$224,234	$215,639
4	Cost of Sales	$163,756	$141,048	$131,376
5	Research and Development	$14,236	$11,581	$10,045
6	Selling, General and administrative	$16,705	$15,261	$14,194
7	Non-Operating Income	$5,245	$5,068	$2,804
8	Interest Expenses	$3,240	$2,323	$1,456
9	Taxable Income	72,903	64,089	$61,372

Individuals need to understand that taxable income is more than the salary they earn at work. Any compensation received will be included in taxable income. Some examples of unusual income that is included in taxable earnings include debts forgiven by creditors or lenders, payments for jury service, gifts, unemployment benefits offered by the government, and strike benefits.

Tax credits reduce the amount of tax that an individual will pay, while tax exemptions and deductions reduce the individual's taxable earnings. The Internal Revenue Code Section 63 defines the items in US accounting that are considered "taxable income." The sources of "gross revenue" are defined by Section 61.

Differences Between Payroll Taxes for Employees and Employers

Both employers and employees are responsible for paying payroll taxes. Some taxes must be paid by an employer, and others by their employee. The taxes are calculated and then paid to the appropriate agency based on the employee's taxable earnings.

Here is the list of state and federal taxes paid by each party:

Employer-only:
- Federal unemployment taxes

- State unemployment taxes

- Local Taxes

Only Employees:
- Federal income tax

- Tax on State Income

- Local Taxes

Employee and employer:
- Tax on Social Security

- Medicare tax

What Is the Employee's Taxable Income?

Employers use the taxable income of an employee to calculate how much tax they owe each agency. The tax that you pay on your taxable income includes any money earned by performing job duties, such as wages, commissions, or tips.

Benefits from employers are not usually taxed. These can include healthcare benefits, child care, or benefits for dependents. Taxable fringe benefits include personal use of company cars or life insurance up to a specified amount.

While the current laws mandate that employees and employers pay taxes to federal and state agencies on their income, deductions may be voluntary or contribute to employee benefits. Federal and state laws impose taxes on income, but they do not correspond to payroll deductions.

Examples of deductions are:

- Health insurance premiums

- Life insurance premiums

- Retirement plan contributions (401k)

- Stock purchases by employees

- Food, uniforms, and other expenses related to the job

Breakdown of employee taxes and payroll taxes

Payroll taxes are deducted each pay period and contribute towards certain benefits provided by the federal government or states. Taxes are calculated based on gross wages. Gross wages are defined as how much money an employee earns over a period of time, such as a two-week pay cycle or according to whichever payment schedule the employer mandates.

The net, or take-home wage, is the remaining amount after tax and deductions. Employees receive a detailed record at the end of each year of all taxes paid.

Taxes Employee Pay

The current amount of payroll tax that an employee must pay is:

Tax on Social Security

The Social Security Tax covers the employee's pension, disability, or survivor benefits. Social Security taxes and Medicare taxes are both mandated by the Federal Insurance Contributions Act, or Self-Employment Contributions Act. The taxes are usually drawn when an employee retires or becomes disabled, or to provide a benefit for widows and widowers.

Medicare Tax

The Medicare tax is part of FICA, a payroll tax that pays for medical insurance benefits. It's a federal program that provides health coverage to workers after reaching a certain level of age. Hospital insurance, medical coverage, prescription drug coverage, and advantage plans are all included in these benefits. Employees earning more than $200,000 per year are subject to an extra 0.9% deduction from their earned income.

Federal income tax

The US federal tax is collected based on an employee's total gross wage, their exemptions, and their filing status. The tax rates may change year-to-year, and the employees' tax brackets can vary. This will affect how much federal income tax is deducted from every paycheck.

Tax on State Income

Some employees are required to pay taxes in the state in which they reside and work. In some states, wages are not taxed (Alaska and Florida), while in others, the tax rate may vary.

Local Taxes

In some states, employees may be required to pay local taxes. The tax amount is usually paid in the form of a percentage of a salary or federal, state, or flat taxes. Local taxes can vary by city, and they may be used to fund school districts or community improvements and parks.

Taxes Employers Pay

Employers pay and withhold all payroll taxes for their employees before reporting the amounts to the IRS or other agencies. Some employers are the only ones who pay certain taxes.

This is the list of state and federal taxes that employers pay:

- **The Federal Unemployment Tax Act:** This tax is paid by employers to the federal government in order to help states pay unemployment benefits to employees who lose their jobs without consent. This tax is based on the first $7,00 of an employee's wage.

- **State unemployment taxes**: unlike federal unemployment taxes, states fund the majority of unemployment benefits. Based on the quantity of unemployment claims, employers are responsible for paying this tax. It may be adjusted from one year to another.

- Local taxes may be different from one state or municipality to another and can go towards city improvement or education.

Taxes Both Parties Pay

The FICA (Federal Insurance Contributions Act) tax is paid by both employees and employers. The employer has a number of payroll tax obligations, including withholding taxes and paying them. The payment of FICA tax is very important. FICA taxes have a unique feature in that they require both an employee to pay a portion of taxes and an employer to pay corresponding taxes.

FICA taxes withheld from an employee's wages:

1. Social Security Tax: 6.2 Percent

2. The "normal" Medicare tax is 1.45 percent.

3. The additional Medicare tax of 0.9 percent is now in effect for employees earning more than $200,000.

Employers are also required to pay a portion of Social Security taxes and Medicare.

FICA tax owed by employers:

- Social Security Tax: 6.2 Percent

- 1.45 percent Medicare tax (the "regular" Medicare tax).

You can see that the amount you are required to deduct from the wages of your employees for social security and Medicare taxes is exactly the same. Different rules apply to employees receiving tips. The employer's share of the additional Medicare tax, which is 0.9 percent on employees earning high salaries, does not exist.

Chapter 3

Understanding Your W-2 Form: Breakdown

Understanding Your W-2

The W-2 is one of the most important tax forms that you will receive. Your employer issued this document, which includes information on your salary for the previous year as well as the amount of tax withheld. Understanding the meaning of each line on your W-2 is crucial to submitting your return correctly and getting your maximum refund.

This chapter offers a detailed breakdown of the form. Discover what is considered taxable income, how to calculate additional Medicare wages, and where you can get your Social Security and Medicare tax.

When you receive your paycheck, it's likely that you won't pay much attention to anything other than the net pay—the amount deposited in your account.

Many taxpayers only consider the amount of money taken from their paychecks during tax season.

It can be difficult to understand all the information that is included on a Form W-2. You should understand how the numbers on Form W-2 affect your bottom line, whether you are typing them into your tax software or giving it to a professional. What you need to understand about your current Form W-2.

If you're an employee, your employer will give you a W-2 form. If you are an independent contractor, then you will receive a different form (Form 1099). The form you receive during tax season shouldn't be a surprise.

If you received at least $600 of cash or cash equivalent in the past year, which includes taxable benefits, your employer is required to issue you a W-2. No matter how many or how long you worked, it doesn't really matter. Your employer must report if you have received more than $600 as an employee, whether you work part-time, full-time, seasonally, or permanently.

The $600 rule has two exceptions:

- No matter how much money you received, if any taxes were withheld (including those for Social Security and Medicare), your employer is required to issue you a W-2.

- Your employee will issue a Form W-2 to you regardless of how much money you received. If you were subject to withholding, but had only claimed one withholding allowance on Form W-4 or had not claimed exemptions from withholding in Form W-4, then you are still subjected.

You will receive three copies from your employer. You will receive three copies of Form W-2 in your mailbox.

- Copy B is the form used to report federal income taxes. It is usually filed along with your federal tax return, unless you are filing electronically. You must give Copy B to your preparer in this case. However, it is not necessary to send it to the IRS.

- Copy 2 is to be used for reporting your state, local, or municipal income tax. It is filed with the appropriate tax authorities.

- Copy C is to be kept for your records.

- It's a lot. You can get your forms electronically if you prefer less paper and if your employer uses a system that is suitable. You must consent to this. Your employer cannot send Form W-2 electronically to an employee who has not agreed to or revoked their consent.

- Your Form W-2 should reflect the wages you received during the calendar year. If you worked between Dec. 18, 20, 22, and January 3, 2023 and were paid Dec. 25, 2022, and Jan. 10, respectively, you would receive two W-2 forms: one for each of the days in 2022.

What if you were paid Jan. 3, 2023, but worked between Dec. 18, 2022, and Dec. 31, 2022? Your 2023 W-2 will include all of these wages.

The form is recognizable by its typical appearance:

What is on the Form W-2? Take a look.

a Employee's social security number			Safe, accurate, FAST! Use	Visit the IRS website at www.irs.gov/efile.
OMB No. 1545-0008		1 Wages, tips, other compensation		2 Federal income tax withheld
b Employer identification number (EIN)				
c Employer's name, address, and ZIP code	3 Social security wages		4 Social security tax withheld	
	5 Medicare wages and tips		6 Medicare tax withheld	
	7 Social security tips		8 Allocated tips	
d Control number	9		10 Dependent care benefits	
e Employee's first name and initial Last name Suff.	11 Nonqualified plans		12a See instructions for box 12	
	13 Statutory employee Retirement plan Third-party sick pay		12b	
	14 Other		12c	
			12d	
f Employee's address and ZIP code				
15 State Employer's state ID number	16 State wages, tips, etc.	17 State income tax	18 Local wages, tips, etc.	19 Local income tax	20 Locality name

Form W-2 Wage and Tax Statement **2024** Department of the Treasury—Internal Revenue Service

Copy B—To Be Filed With Employee's FEDERAL Tax Return.
This information is being furnished to the Internal Revenue Service.

Figure 1: Screenshot of 2024 W-2 Form by KPE/IRS

Personal Information:

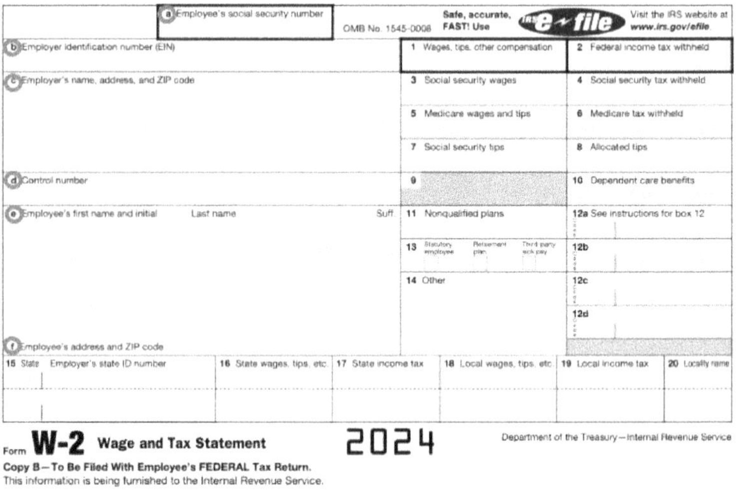

Figure 2: W-2 Showing the Personal information

On the left-hand side, you can enter your personal information.

Box A is where your Social Security Number is reported. In the past, your SSN was displayed in full. This is no longer true. Now, your employee can truncate the SSN in your W-2 copies. As a result, asterisks or Xs may substitute for the first five numbers of the nine-digit SSN.

Box B is where you report your employer's EIN, which is the equivalent of an SSN.

Box C will show your employer's legal address. This is the legal address of your employer, which may or may not be the place where you work.

A control number is a number that your employer uses internally or by the payroll department. It's no big deal if your employer does not use control numbers.

Box D will simply be blank.

Boxes E and F are grouped together on the W-2 form. Box E should contain your full name, which is the same as on your Social Security card. You may need to fill out a new Form W-2 if your name does not appear exactly the same as on your Social Security card. The Form W-2 should not include honorifics or prefixes such as "Dr." or "Esq." Although there is a box to enter suffixes, like "Jr." or "Sr.," these shouldn't appear unless they are on your Social Security card.

You'll need a new Social Security card if your name changes. The name on the Form W-2 will still be the same as the one on the card you have until you get a corrected copy.

You will find your mailing address in Box F. Notify your employer if your address is incorrect. You won't require a new W-2, but they must update their records.

Wages and Withholding

a Employee's social security number				OMB No. 1545-0008	Safe, accurate, FAST! Use	*e~file*	Visit the IRS website at www.irs.gov/efile.

b Employer identification number (EIN)		1 Wages, tips, other compensation	2 Federal income tax withheld
c Employer's name, address, and ZIP code		3 Social security wages	4 Social security tax withheld
		5 Medicare wages and tips	6 Medicare tax withheld
		7 Social security tips	8 Allocated tips
d Control number		9	10 Dependent care benefits
e Employee's first name and initial Last name Suff		11 Nonqualified plans	12a See instructions for box 12
		13 Statutory employee Retirement plan Third party sick pay	12b
		14 Other	12c
			12d
f Employee's address and ZIP code			
15 State Employer's state ID number	16 State wages, tips, etc.	17 State income tax	18 Local wages, tips, etc. 19 Local income tax 20 Locality name

Form **W-2** Wage and Tax Statement **2024** Department of the Treasury—Internal Revenue Service

Copy B—To Be Filed With Employee's FEDERAL Tax Return.
This information is being furnished to the Internal Revenue Service.

Figure 3: Screenshot of where you record your financial data.

The W-2 form also has numbered boxes. This is where you record your financial data.

Box 1: This is where your total taxable wage or salary is reported for federal income tax purposes. This number includes all of your wages, salaries, tips, bonuses, and other taxable compensation. This includes, for example, fringe benefits like group term life insurance. Box 1 excludes pre-tax benefits such as contributions to a 403(b), 401(k), or health insurance. The amount from Box 1 is reported on Line 7 of your Form 1040 or 1040A, or on Line 1 of Form 1040EZ. If you have several W-2 forms, add up the Box 1 amounts and enter the total.

Box 2: This part shows the total amount that your employer deducted from your pay for federal income tax. This is the total amount of federal income taxes that you paid throughout the year. The amount in Box 2 will be reported on line 62 of the Form 1040 or on line 36 of the Form 1040A. It is also reported on line 7 of Form 1040EZ. Add up the Box 2 figures on all W-2 forms, just like you did for your income.

Box 3: This part shows your total earnings subject to Social Security tax. This number is calculated without any payroll deductions. Therefore, the figure in box 3 may be higher than that reported in box 1. If you earn a lot of money, it could be lower than the box-to-box amount. The maximum Social Security wage base cannot exceed your wages. In 2022, the amount was $147,000. The cap applies even if you work more than one job.

Box 4: This displays the total Social Security taxes collected for the year. Social Security taxes, unlike federal income taxes, are calculated using a flat rate. The rate is 6.2%. The total in box 4 should equal the total in box 3 multiplied by 6.2%. Since you shouldn't have more Social Security deductions than the maximum wage basis times 6.2%, the amount in Box 4 for 2022 shouldn't be more than $9,114.

Box 5: This will show the wages that are subject to Medicare tax. Medicare taxes do not usually include pretax deductions. Medicare taxes are not capped, unlike Social Security. The amount in box 5 could be higher than those in boxes 1 or 3.

Box 6: This indicates the amount of Medicare tax withheld during the year. Medicare wages are taxed flat at 1.45%. This means that for most taxpayers, the number at box 6 is equal to the number at box 5 multiplied by 1.45%. Regardless of their filing status or whether they receive pay from another employer, you must withhold an additional 0.9% Medicare tax from the wages of people making over $200,000.

Box 7: This shows the tip income that you have reported to your employer. If you did not report any tips, the box will be blank. If you have no pre-tax benefit, the amounts in boxes 7 and 3 will add up to those in box 1. They may also equal the amount shown in Box 5 if pre-tax benefits are received. The total of Boxes 7 and 3 must not exceed the $118,500 Social Security base wage. Box 7's amount is already included in Box 1.

Box 8: This box reports any tip income you receive from your employer. This amount does not appear in Boxes 1, 3, or 5. You must instead add this amount to your taxable wage on Form 1040, Line 7. Then you will need to calculate your Social Security and Medicare tax, including the tip income, by using IRS **Form 4137**.

Box **9**: This part was used in the past to report any advance earned income credit. Advance-earned income credit has ended since 2010. This box should be empty. Employers who anticipate that an employee will qualify for earned-income credit make advance EIC payments.

Box 10: Your employer must report all benefits paid to you under a dependent-care assistance program. This includes any that exceeds $5,000 (if this value exceeds $5,000, the excess is reported in boxes 1, 3, and 5). The amounts less than $5,000 that are paid through a qualified plan will be considered nontaxable.

Box 11: This will reflect amounts distributed to you from your employer's nonqualified deferred compensation plan; this amount is taxable. Don't confuse this with the amounts you contributed. That shows up in box 12.

Box 12: This is where all the information for Form W-2 is gathered. You'll find all sorts of codes here: If there are more items than four to be reported in box 12, your employer can use a separate form W-2 to declare these additional items. Box 12 does not include all income that is taxable.

Box 12 Codes

Here is a list of the most common codes.

C. Taxable cost for group term life insurance above $50,000

D--H, S, Y, AA, BB, and Elective deferrals and designated Roth contributions

J. Nontaxable sick pay

L. Substantiated Employee Business Expense Reimbursements (nontaxable).

P. Directly paid moving expenses reimbursed to a US Armed Forces member

R. Employer contributions to an Archer MSA

V. Income from non-statutory stock options.

W. Contributions from your employer to your health saving account

Y. Deferrals pursuant to a nonqualified deferred-compensation plan under section 409A

Z. Income under a nonqualified deferred compensation plan that fails to satisfy section 409A

Code DD. Cost of employer-sponsored or employer-paid health insurance. This amount is not taxed to you.

Code DD: Cost of employer-sponsored or employer-paid health insurance. This amount is not taxed to you.

Box 13: Three check boxes are displayed in Box 13. If any of the following situations are applicable to you as an employee, they will be crossed out.

You are a statutory worker. You are a statutory employee. However, they are subject to Social Security tax withholdings and Medicare tax, so boxes 3 through 6 must be filled in.

During the tax year, you participated in the retirement plan of your employer. It could be a 401(k) plan or a 403(b) plan. Or it could be a SEP-IRA, SIMPLE IRA, or other type of pension. If you are a participant in a retirement program, your ability to deduct contributions from a traditional IRA could be limited based on your income. Consult an accountant or tax professional if the box is checked.

Instead of receiving your sick pay directly from the employer, you received third-party sickness pay through your third-party insurance plan. Sick pay does not appear in your Box 1 wage, but it is subject to Social Security taxes and Medicare.

Box 14: Your employer can report more tax information in this box. You should give a short description of any amounts reported in Box 14. This box can be used to report union dues or employer-paid tuition, as well as contributions after tax made to a retirement account. Certain employers report state and local taxes, such as State Disability Insurance premiums (SDI), in Box 14. If you itemized on Schedule A, state disability insurance premiums could be deducted as part of your deductions for state and local taxes. Union dues might also be deducted as a miscellaneous deduction.

State and local taxes

You will find your state and local tax numbers at the bottom of Form W-2.

Box 15: This contains your employer's tax identification number and state. This box, along with boxes 16–17, will be empty if you live in a state that does not require reporting. You will see more than one box if you have multiple withholdings from different states. With the increase in remote work, your employer may need to report information from more than two localities or states. In this case, you will receive multiple Form W-2s that will include personal identification information but not items included on other Form W-2s.

Box 16 will show the total amount of taxable wages for state tax purposes.

Box 17 is the total of the state income tax withheld. If you live in Pennsylvania, for example, and your state has a flat-rate tax, you can check to see if you have the correct amount of withholding by multiplying box 16 by that flat rate.

Box 19 will indicate the name of any local, city, or state tax that you have paid.

Box 20 will list the local, state, or city tax that was reported in Box 19.

Who uses a W-2 form?

W-2 forms are used by the IRS, state and local authorities, and employers. This is a brief description of the way each group uses it:

Employer

Employers are required to submit copies of the W-2 form to the Social Security Administration (SSA), the IRS, and state and local tax authorities. This form is used to report Federal Insurance Contributions Act (FICA) taxes. Employers who pay their employees more than $600 a year must submit this form. The W-2 is used by employers to record the salaries they pay their employees and any taxes that are deducted from the employee's paycheck.

Employee

Each year, an employee completes their tax return using Form W-2. Employees must fill out the correct wage and tax data as shown on the forms to complete their tax returns. The form is usually given to employees in multiples: one to be used to submit a federal tax return, another to report a local or state return, and a third for personal records.

For those who worked multiple jobs in the tax year prior, a separate W-2 is issued for each one. Collect all of your W-2s if you have multiple jobs so that you can correctly file your taxes. You may need to use different tax forms if you are self-employed or a contractor employee. It's best to check before you file.

IRS

IRS W-2 Form is used to collect data and determine how much a person owes or if they qualify for a refund. The IRS also makes use of these forms to track all employee wages on a national level. The IRS also uses these forms to track earnings and tax liabilities for all citizens. The IRS will conduct an audit if the W-2 income does not match what is reported in the tax return of the employee.

State and Local Tax Authorities

In addition to federal income taxes, nearly all local and state governments require their residents to pay personal income taxes. Similar to the IRS's Form W2, state and city tax authorities also use it to calculate tax amounts at both the local and state levels. Form W-2 helps local and state governments keep track of the income and tax payments of residents.

Common W-2 Errors

You should be on the lookout for mistakes now that you know what your W-2 form is made up of. Errors do happen, whether it's because of simple clerical errors or problems on the employer's side with reporting payroll data. Double-check these common mistakes on W-2s:

1. The name or SSN is missing or incorrect.

The IRS requires employers to correct any errors in the employee's Social Security Number (SSN). The IRS requires employers to correct errors in an employee's name or Social Security number (SSN).

Employees who have changed their names due to divorce or marriage are required to submit a Form W-4. If the employee's name is different from the one on their Social Security card, they must check box 4 of the Form W-4.

The IRS requires that Form W-2s for employees and Form 1095 Cs match the information on their social security cards. If, for example, an employee's social security card has a hyphenated name but the same name is not hyphenated in their Form W-2 and Form 1095-C, then this will be flagged.

2. The name or address of the employer is incorrect.

If you need to change the employer address, you should use Form 8822-B. A Form 8822-B is needed to change the employer's address. This type of information cannot be corrected using Form W-3c.

3. The employee's address is incorrect.

If the IRS or employer need to contact an employee, they should provide a mailing address. If the Form W-2 contains an error relating to the employee's home address, the employer has three choices:

- Give the employee a corrected W-2 form with "reissued" printed on it.

- Send the original W-2 form to the correct employee's address.

- Fill out a W-2c indicating the correct address and any other information that is correct.

4. HSA Contributions Exceeded

The employer can correct the error if there have been excess contributions made to the employee's Health Savings Accounts (HSA) that exceed the maximum annual contribution amounts for 2019 for either self-only coverage for the employee or family coverage.

- First, the employer can request that the financial institution return any excess funds and refund the amount to the employee. The employer can then issue a W-2c showing a reduction in the amount in box 12, code W.

- The employer can choose to include the excess contributions in the taxable wages shown on Form W-2 boxes 1, 3, and 5. In boxes 4 and 6, the Social Security and Medicare taxes due on the excess amount are shown. Form W-2c is required if this amount was not correctly recorded on the Form W-2.

5. Excess Contributions to the Qualified Pension Plan

If you have excess contributions to retirement plans that are qualified, such as 403(b), then these contributions should be reported not on Form W-2 but rather on Form 1099R.

6. FSA Contributions Exceeding Pretax

If an employee has exceeded the annual limit of the 2019 FSA contribution pretax, the excess amount should be refunded and recorded in Form W-2c boxes 1, 2, and 5 as taxable wage.

Please be aware that, if you do not make this correction, your employer will be held responsible for the Social Security and Medicare taxes not deducted and must pay this amount. The employer is also responsible for any federal tax or additional Medicare tax that was not withheld. The employer can avoid federal income tax and additional Medicare tax liabilities by recording the excess or obtaining Form 4469 directly from the employee.

7. Incorrect Amount Reported in Box 12, Code D

In some cases, the value of employer-sponsored coverage can be reported incorrectly. To correct Box 12 Code DD, a Form W-2c must be completed. A penalty of $270 can be assessed per Form W-2 if this is not done.

8. Incorrect EIN or Tax Year

Errors in Form W-2, such as errors relating to the employer identification number or the tax year, can cause employers a lot of time-consuming issues. A penalty is assessed for EIN or tax year reporting mistakes. The process of correcting an EIN or a tax year involves two steps.

Step 1: Prepare the Forms W-2c and W-3c using the previously reported information.

- In box b, enter the wrong EIN or tax year.

- The money amounts that were originally reported in the previous column.

- In the column for the corrected amount, enter zeros.

Step 2: Fill out the Forms W-2c and W-3c correctly.

- In the previous column, enter zero for the amount.

- In the column for the correct amounts, show the initial money amounts.

- Give employees a copy of Form W-2c. File FormsW-2c and FormsW-3c at the SSA.

9. Error Withholding Federal Income Tax/Additional Medicare Tax

If adjustments to a W-2 form are required for the reporting of federal income tax or Additional Medicare Tax withheld, the Internal Revenue Service (IRS) will not approve them unless they are deemed "administrative." If the amounts listed on Form 941 do not correspond to the amounts withheld, the error may be remedied.

10. Excess FICA/Social Security/Medicare Withholding

When they receive a Form W-2 showing excess FICA withholding, employers need to know the corrective process. When there is an excess of
Social Security/Medicare Withholding (FICA), the IRS expects employers to complete these steps:

- The excess FICA should be refunded, and a W-2c form with the correct amount withheld for FICA should be issued.

- Refund any overpayments of FICA taxes to employees.

- You can request a refund or adjustment for Social Security and Medicare overpayments by the employee and the employer if the employee does not want to claim the refund on their personal income tax returns.

Form W2 Penalties

You now know the most common W-2 errors. It's also important that you understand what penalties can be imposed for incorrect W-2 forms. Since W-2 errors have a significant impact on tax refunds and payments, the IRS takes them very seriously. The IRS has outlined the penalties associated with Form W-2.

Large businesses that have gross receipts exceeding $5 million

Time Returns Filed/Provided	Not More Than 30 Days Late	31 Days Late – August 1	After August 1 – Not At All	Intentional Disregard
Due 1/1/2020 – 12/31/2020	$50 per return or statement – $556,500 maximum	$110 per return or statement – $1,669,500 maximum	$270 per return or statement – $3,339,000 maximum	$550 per return or statement – No limitation

Small businesses with gross receipts less than $5 million

Time Returns Filed/Provided	Not More Than 30 Days Late	31 Days Late – August 1	After August 1 – Not At All	Iintentional Disregard
Due 1/1/2020 – 12/31/2020	$50 per return or statement – $194,500 maximum	$110 per return or statement – $556,500 maximum	$270 per return or statement – $1,113,000 maximum	$550 per return or statement – No limitation

How to Obtain a W2 Form from Employers

If you changed jobs in the past year, you must have a W-2, also called a Wage and Tax Statement, from your previous employer to file your taxes.

Companies send W-2s to all employees at the start of every year. These W-2s include details about their previous earnings and taxes. You must get a W-2 if you changed jobs within the last year.

Your former employer must send you a copy before January 31. If your W-2 is still unaccounted for or missing by the end of January, you might need to take action. You can take these simple steps to ensure you get your W-2 in time.

1. **Date Check**

Watch the calendar and be aware of important dates. You have until the 31st of January to get your W-2 from your former employer. It may not arrive before the first of February. The IRS says that you must receive your W-2 no later than February 14.

2. **If you have moved, change your address.**

You should fill out the change of address form at your local United States Post Office if your current and former addresses have changed. You will need to wait between seven and ten days after submitting the form before USPS can process your request. Mail should arrive at your new home within this time frame. You may have received your W-2 from your old employer if you failed to complete this form when moving.

3. Search your email

Your former employer may have sent you tax documents in digital format. You can search your spam and inbox for emails indicating that your tax documents have been prepared. The notice will usually include a link that takes you to a safe online platform where you can download and access important documents, such as your W-2.

4. Contact your former employer.

Contact your former employer if you still haven't received a W-2 by January 31. You can contact the human resources department of the previous company to inquire about your W-2 status and confirm that they have the correct address. The form may have been mailed but got lost or sent to the incorrect address. Call your previous manager if the company doesn't have an HR department. To save time, offer to collect your W-2 personally.

5. Payroll administrator

Call or email your company's payroll administrator if they use a third party to handle payroll. Confirm the address that is on record for you and request a copy of the form if it was mailed but hasn't arrived.

6. Contact the IRS.

Call the IRS at 1-800-829-1040 if you are unable to contact your former employers; they haven't responded to your request, and you still didn't receive your W-2 before the deadline. You can locate the employer identification number on old paystubs and W-2s. You may also be asked to provide information like your Social Security number, contact details of the company, an estimate of earnings, and dates that you worked there. The IRS then reminds your former employer to send your W-2.

Tips If You Can't Get Your W-2 From Your Previous Employer

If you cannot get a W-2 form from your former employer, here are some tips to help.

You still have to file your tax return if you believe that you won't receive your W-2 before the deadline of April 15. There are a couple of options you can take to avoid IRS penalties:

- To request an extension, submit Form 4868, Application for Automatic Extension of Time to Filing U.S. You can ask for an extension by submitting Form 4868, Individual Income Tax Return. You will have an additional six months to submit your tax returns, but you must pay on time. You must include your estimate for how much you owe in taxes and the payment.

- You can file without a W-2 if you don't expect to get a W-2 from your former employer, e.g., if they have closed their doors. Instead, you may submit Form 4852. Substitute Form W-2 Wage and Tax Statement with your return. Estimate your income and withholdings using the last pay stub you received from the company. Then, complete Form 4852. You can correct errors if you received your W-2 before submitting the 4852.

You can download these forms from the IRS website and submit them by April 1. Filing a replacement form or requesting an extension can delay the processing of your tax return. However, it will stop the IRS from fining you for unfiled or overdue taxes.

Chapter 4

Preparing for the w2 Form

In the previous chapter of this book, you have understood different parts of the W-2 form. Now is the time to prepare for it.

The most important part of the W-2 process is collecting and verifying the employee's information. The omission or error of required information can cause problems and delays. It could even lead to IRS penalties.

Start by collecting key information on each employee that worked in the year. Documentation must be provided, whether they are team members who currently work in your company or former employees.

Gathering the following required information is step one in creating W-2s.

1. Employee Information

To complete W-2 correctly, you will need to have accurate information about your employees. You should collect the employee's full name, Social Security number, home address and other information that your business uses to identify them, like an employee ID. The correct identification of employees helps to match the W-2 forms with the appropriate individual. Verify that the employee's name matches their Social Security record. Update employee data periodically by reviewing and updating it.

You should also keep track of marital status and other factors that may affect the tax calculation. These include multiple jobs, pre-tax deductibles, garnishments or any other situation. You may need to change tax withholding if, for example, an employee marries and claims additional allowances or changes his last name on the Form W-4. W-2s should reflect any changes to taxable earnings, such as a reduction or an increase.

2. Payroll Records

You will also need to keep detailed payroll records of the whole tax year. Included in this are total wages, withheld federal taxes, Social Security, Medicare, 401 (k) contributions and premiums paid for health insurance, Flexible Spending Account contributions, reported tips, non-cash payments and reimbursements above the allowed amount, as well as third party sick pay and taxable fringe benefits.

Check your annual payroll reports for accuracy in reporting all taxes, adjustments, and deductions that affect each employee's pay. Check that employees' life insurance premiums are not included in federally taxable wages. Verify that the pretax benefits for transportation are correctly coded as nontaxable income when used to pay for parking, transit or vanpool passes. To calculate the correct W-2 wages for the year, any corrections made to previous pay periods must also be taken into account.

Using accurate payroll records, you can accurately complete all the boxes on W-2s relating to employee wages, taxes and other benefits.

3. Companies Information

You will also need to print the company name, address, phone number and federal employer identification number (EIN) on W-2s before you fill in employee specific amounts. Included in this information are the name of your company, its address, telephone number, and EIN (federal employer identification number). The information is entered in the "Employer information" box at the top.

Check that the company information, such as name, EIN and address are up-to-date before ordering or printing preprinted forms. To avoid any issues with reconciling the W-2 wage amount to that reported in 941 or 940 tax returns, you should make sure your employer data matches exactly. Use the EIN linked to payroll tax payments made from your company's bank account throughout the entire year.

After gathering initial information, it is imperative to confirm that everything is accurate, current and aligned on all platforms. Consider carefully examining details to determine if there are any areas that need correction, such as:

Wrong or Outdated Employee Data Errors

During manual data entry, such as paperwork transpositions and outdated records, errors can occur. Check that the information collected matches W-4s and I-9s. Also, check official documents, signatures, and other documentation. Inconsistencies should be flagged for further investigation against the source documents.

Wrong calculation of benefits, taxes or deductions. An incorrect set-up of payroll deductions may cause figures to be distorted. Verify, for example, that garnishments are in accordance with court orders and 401(k), contributions match set percentages. Also, make sure systems take into account the latest IRS tax tables. Validate totals manually.

Unaccounted for Compensation Pay

Compensation Pay that is not reconciled should include bonuses, commissions and tips. These are reported by other sources besides payroll.

There are multiple versions of names.

Verify accuracy by noticing small variations between platforms, such as "Will Wilson", "William Wilson", etc.

Suspicious Number Sequences

Recording mistakes can be identified by checking for repeated digits, or numbers shared between workers.

How to Note Errors

Double verification and cross-referencing are the best ways to pinpoint any discrepancies. Validation checks should be rigorous, such as the following:

1. Cross-Platform review

Pull payroll files for employees and check independently that W-4/I-9 information matches the corresponding draft W-2. Compare salaries, personal data and deductions. Payroll registers, HR database, and payment records can be used to complete direct accuracy walkthroughs for each person.

2. Colleague and Manager Confirmation email

Send a confirmation email to the organization's leaders, asking them for their approval. Include a list of expected salaries and details about your direct report. Send the same confirmations to your staff and ask them to confirm their name, SSN, wage to be paid on W-2s, as well as any amendment requests.

3. Identification Authentication

Refer to official identifications such as passports, SSNs or marriage licenses. Compare employee names, SSNs and addresses directly with pending W-2 preparation data. This technique also checks for fake documentation.

To ensure compliance, it is important to follow confirmation steps. If data that is crucial for federal tax calculations and reporting, as well as hourly wages are not aligned and corrected promptly before W-2 completion, an IRS audit could be initiated.

In addition, many states have a strict policy against filing incorrect W-2 forms that reflect inaccurate tax amounts, particularly in the case of unemployment insurance or disability claims. Reporting incorrect information causes backlogs in processing, which delays tax refunds for employees. By certifying details, you can avoid these complications and delays.

Consider the attention to detail as an insurance policy. Early detection of problems and correcting mistakes before deadlines gives you ample time to react. Shortcuts increase the likelihood of payroll mistakes, which can lead to more costly resolutions in the future. Spend time now to ensure smoother W-2 workflows.

Compile your final W-2 file after you have resolved discrepancies, and ensured data integrity between systems. Check that the dollar amount and stripes are correctly transferred from final payroll totals. Once you have confirmed that your metrics are clean, formalize wage reporting on W-2 forms in either physical or digital form knowing the submissions will accurately reflect employee reality.

Determining Proper W-2 Box Amounts

Calculating the correct amounts for each W-2 box is an essential payroll function. Calculations and rules are used to determine the right amounts in each box.

Federal Income Tax Withholding

The amount of federal income tax that is withheld from the employee's paycheck will be reported in box 2 on their W-2. The amount depends on an employee's filing situation, the number of allowances they claim on their Form W-4 and his or her income. Employers can determine the withholding amounts for each pay period using IRS Publication 15 (also known as Circular E). This publication includes tables that list the withholding amounts based on the employee's income, filing status and the number of allowances claimed.

To determine withholding per pay period, the employer multiplies each amount by the number in the table. If, for example, an employee makes $2,000 bi-monthly, and he claims single allowances with two, then the table indicates that $138 is to be deducted. If you multiply 24 pay periods by a year then the employee should be withholding $138 each pay period. The employer will have to deposit $3,312 into Box 2 on the W-2.

State Income Tax withholding

In Box 17 on Form W-2, you will find the amount of state income tax that has been withheld. State income tax laws determine the amount of withholding. The IRS has tables that are similar to those used by many states. Some states employ a percentage-based method.

A state might require a withholding of 5% on gross income. A $50,000 employee would be required to withhold $2,500 for state taxes: $50,000 x 5.5% = $2,000. The $2,500 is reported at Box 17. To calculate the state withholding tax correctly, employers must understand each state's rules.

Local Income Tax withholding

Some municipalities or cities impose a local income tax to employees who work there. The local tax is shown in box 19 on the W-2. Local tax rules are required to be adhered to in order to calculate the correct amount to withhold for each pay period.

Social Security and Medicare Wages

The W-2 forms include boxes 3 and 5, which report Social Security wages and Medicare earnings, respectively. These boxes include both pre-tax deductions, such as health insurance and retirement plans contributions.

Social Security's wage base for 2023 was $160 200, which means that only the first $160 200 of an employee's salary is subject to Social Security Tax of 6.2%. There is no limit on the wage base for Medicare tax. Medicare taxes are 1.45% of all earnings.

If an employee earns $80,000 a year, they would report $80,000 in box 3 (up to the Social Security wage limits) and the entire $80,000 in box 5 (no limit). The employee's Social Security tax and Medicare is calculated using these boxes.

Social Security/Medicare Taxes Withheld

The boxes 4 and 6 show the amount of Social Security and Medicare tax deducted from an employee's wage. The tax rate (6.2% Social Security and 1.45% Medicare) is multiplied by the employee's wage amount, subject to wage limitations.

On $80,000 of wages, the Social Security Tax is 6.2% (limited by $160,200 as a wage base). The Medicare tax is 1.45% on $80,000.

In this case, Box 4 will report the $4,960 Social Security withheld, and Box 6 $1,160 Medicare withheld. When calculating the amounts, make sure that you are using the correct tax rates for each year.

The Cost of Health Insurance

In Box 12 with Code DD, the cost of health coverage provided by the employer is shown. The employee is informed of the cost of the health insurance coverage for the purposes of calculating individual responsibility payments under the Affordable Care Act.

If, for example, an employer covers 80% of a $500 health insurance premium paid by the employee, then the employer will pay $400 per month. The employer spent $4,800 for the entire year ($400 divided by 12 months). The $4,800 amount is entered in Box 12 under Code DD. This amount should be reported in Box 12 with Code DD.

Contributions to Retirement Plans

W-2 Box 13 reports contributions to retirement plans offered by employers, like 401(k)s. Code D is used to report pre-tax deferrals that the employee made from their pay. Code E is for employer matching contributions or non-elective deductions.

If, for example, the employee contributed $10,000 and the employer $5,000 to a 401 (k) plan - box 13 would show D-$10,000 E-50%. The employee will be informed of the total contributions made to retirement for the entire year.

Non-cash Compensation

The employee may have received a wage in another form than cash, such as clothing, goods, or lodging. The fair market value for these non-cash items are reported along with the regular cash wage in boxes 1, 3 and 5. They are reported separately in box 14.

If, for example, an employee earns $45,000 regular wage plus $2,000 in uniforms provided by the employer, boxes 1, 3 and 5 will report $47,000. In Box 14, it would say "Uniforms -- $2,000". The noncash portion is now clearly identifiable, even though it's included in the gross wage.

To prepare accurate W-2s, it is important to track employee compensation and withholdings all year long. The employer must verify regularly that the payroll system is correctly calculating tax and other deductions. As tax laws are updated, tables and rates should be updated. List any benefits that are not monetary.

Compile data from your payroll records at the end of each year to fill in the W-2 boxes. Make sure that the Social Security wage does not exceed this limit. All the amounts should be in line, minus any pre-tax deducted. Check the Social Security and Medicare calculations.

In the appropriate boxes, report health insurance, retirement contributions and non-cash compensation. W-2s must be issued to all employees before the deadline of January 31. File copies of the W-2s with Social Security Administration. This important process is only possible if you keep organized records of your payroll and understand the W-2 reporting requirements. W-2s are used by employees to file tax returns, calculate Social Security benefits and determine their Social Security benefit amounts.

How to file W-2 Forms

The deadline for filing copies of all W-2s with the Social Security Administration is January 31, 2019. You have three options to file those copies of W-2s: either on paper, electronically through the IRS system or through an efiling service.

1. Paper Forms

The paper form is the traditional way to file W-2s. W-3 is a summary form that summarizes all W-2s, as well as the total wages paid during the calendar year. W-2s are attached to the W-3.

Fill out all paper forms carefully, following instructions. Mistakes may delay processing. Ensure that you print clearly and in black ink. W-3s and W-2s should be mailed at the specified address. The paper forms need to be stamped by January 31, 2019.

Paper forms do not require any specialized software, or online filing systems. Manually completing each form can take a lot of time. The mail can also lose paper forms. After processing your paper return, the IRS will email you a confirmation.

2. IRS FIRE System

The IRS has an online service called FIRE, which allows you to electronically file information returns like W-2s. To request permission to electronically file through FIRE, employers must submit Form 4419.

Once the approval is granted, the employer can then follow the instructions and upload W-2 data to the system. Once the FIRE system has been activated, it will verify that there are no errors in your filing and confirm that you have successfully filed. E-filing removes the worry of lost mail. E-filed tax returns are usually processed faster by the IRS. The FIRE system does, however, require that you are familiar with the online federal systems.

3. The Third-Party E-File Providers

Many employers opt to file electronically through third party service providers rather than directly on the IRS FIRE website. Tax1099 ExpressEfile and AccuWage are companies that offer W-2 file services at a cost.

W-2 information is submitted by the employer to the provider electronically or on paper. The provider formats the return and electronically files it with the IRS for the employer. The process is simplified, but the cost increases. Researchers and fee comparisons are important for employers.

Reporting requirements for W-2 Copies

Employers are also required to report to local and state tax authorities in addition to the SSA.

File your State W-2 Form

Many states ask employers to provide copies of W-2s for all employees who live or work in their state. The state can then track the taxes that residents owe. The instructions for filing vary from state to state, including the forms that must be filed, how to submit them and when to do so.

California, for example, requires that you submit Form W-3 along with copies of W-2s to the California Employment Development Department before January 31. In some states, the W-3 is replaced by a different form such as a Withholding Tax Annual Reconciliation. Each state has its own W-2 reporting requirements.

Filing Local W-2

In the case of employees who work for a municipality or city that has a local income tax system, it may be necessary to file copies of W-2s with their local tax office. Employers in New York City, for example, must submit an Annual Reconciliation of Withholding Tax Form and copies of W-2 to the NYC Department of Finance. If you fail to submit your tax forms locally, penalties may apply.

Dates and deadlines

State and local deadlines for submitting W-2 copies to the SSA vary. Others extend into March or February. Some are the same date as January 31, while others go beyond that. Employers who are unable to meet the deadline for filing may request an extension up to 30 calendar days. They can do this by submitting Form 8809. Extensions are not granted automatically.

Tax Penalties for Late or Incorrect Filing

IRS and state agencies may impose substantial penalties on late or incorrectly reported W-2s. Federal penalties for W-2s can exceed $500. State penalties are usually lower. Intentional failure to file may result in much higher penalties. W-2s should be filed accurately, on time, and with complete information by employers.

Employers must also provide each employee their Form W-2 before the deadline. The W-2 is used by employees to accurately file their tax returns. W-2s inform employees of the taxes they have already paid, so that they do not pay again. W-2 data is also needed by employees to be eligible for public assistance and tax credits.

If certain conditions are met, employers can provide W-2s electronically or on paper. W-2s must include all the information that was filed with IRS in order to help taxpayers accurately report their wages, taxes and benefits on their tax returns.

Preparing for the Annual W-2 Reporting

Employers should begin preparing well before the W-2 deadlines. Payroll systems should be updated to reflect any changes in tax rates and laws for the current year. Keep track of employee salaries, taxes, and benefits throughout the year.

Check information returned by benefit providers and third-party sick pay administrators. Verify that the wage amounts reported in quarterly unemployment tax returns are consistent with those of annual wage statements.

For name changes, collect any necessary employee information such as a copy of the Social Security card. Ensure that employee addresses are up-to-date. If the company has more than one location, you can combine data from different payroll systems.

Distribution of W-2s to Employees

Employers must provide W-2 copies to employees before the deadline. W-2s are used by employees to accurately report their wages and taxes on their tax returns. You can choose to distribute W-2s by mail, email or online. If you need replacement copies, we also provide them.

1. Mailing Paper W-2s

The traditional way is to mail a copy of the W-2 by paper to each employee before the deadline on January 31. The W-2 is a detailed report that shows the employee's income, taxes and benefits.

The IRS Form W-2 should be used by employers. Some older obsolete forms might not contain the required reporting boxes. The W-2 form must include all the information that was filed with SSA including federal taxes withheld, Social Security/Medicare wages/taxes and benefit amounts.

Before printing or mailing, double check all information, including names, Social Security numbers and tax/wage figures. If you choose to electronically file your return, print employee copies with black ink. This will make it easier for the scanner to read. Employers should keep photocopies of electronic copies or download them for their records.

Send W-2s in envelopes that clearly state "Important Document Attached" to encourage quick opening. Verify that the employee's address is current before mailing. Consider sending by certified mail, with a return receipt request.

W-2s may be needed by employees who moved during the course of the year. The employer must take reasonable steps to find the employee and deliver the W-2 if a W-2 is returned undeliverable.

2. Email Delivery

Employees can consent to receiving W-2s electronically by email, if they give written permission. The consent can be revoked at any point. Email offers many advantages, including speed, reduced printing and postage costs, and the ability to avoid mail loss.

Employers must verify that employee emails are valid before sending W-2s. Data security is also a concern when sending W-2s via email. W-2 forms contain information that could be used to steal an employee's identity if they are not encrypted.

Employers are advised to implement email security measures such as encryption, multi-factor verification, and secure document watermarking when emailing W-2s. Attachments can be password protected or the password sent in a separate email. Encourage employees to download tax forms from emailed emails using secure networks.

3. Online System Access

A second electronic option allows employees to access W-2s via a company's online portal or payroll software. Downloadable W-2s are available by the 31st of January. Employees can access the W-2 at any time.

Employers must have written permission to provide W-2s electronically. Data security is also a concern with online systems. Make sure you have robust cybersecurity protections in place. You may require an audit trail that shows when employees accessed W-2s.

4. Replace Copies

Employees may need to replace their original W-2 if they have misplaced it. Also, they may request extra copies for their spouses, mortgage lenders or tax preparers. If an employee requests a replacement W-2, employers must comply.

If the employee agrees, replacements can be provided on official paper or electronically. Employers can charge a reasonable amount for more than two copies of the replacement form per year.

During the tax filing season, employees often request replacement W-2s as they prepare their returns. To respond to requests efficiently, follow these steps:

- Keep W-2 records for employers at least four years.

- Print out forms and keep electronic files readily accessible.

- Specific staff should be designated to deal with W-2 replacement requests.

- Verify the identity/authority or the person requesting the W-2.

- Set a reasonable turnaround for fulfilling requests.

- Consider batching large volumes of requests during peak periods.

- Remind your employees to store copies safely once they have been received.

Employees are responsible for keeping W-2s safe and minimizing requests. While employers will provide replacements, it is the employees' responsibility to keep them secure. Remind them to keep their W-2 and tax records for as long as possible, make copies of the forms for dependents/spouses, track any electronic downloads.

W-2 Distribution for Special Situations

Some employee situations require special treatment for their W-2.

Deceased Employees: The W-2 form must be provided to the estate of the deceased employee or their surviving spouse. It is acceptable to send a cover letter expressing condolences.

Terminated employees: Employees who separate during the year should still receive their W-2. Verify that the mailing address is correct.

New Hires: Even if they join late in the calendar year, employees still receive a W-2 that only reports their wages, taxes, and benefits.

Audits: If the IRS corrects an employee's W-2 after an audit, you should issue a corrected W-2 that is marked "amended."

Identity Theft: Special procedures are in place if the employee has been a victim of W-2 identity fraud. It may be necessary to issue new secured W-2s.

Nonresident aliens: Those with F, M, Q, or J visas are subject to certain restrictions regarding electronic delivery of W-2s.

Employers should keep track of which employees have received their W-2s or accessed them, regardless of the method used to deliver them. If you suspect that an employee has not received his or her tax form, follow up. The W-2 contains important income information that employees need. W-2s that are complete, accurate, and delivered on time foster good employee relations while also demonstrating compliance with the law.

How to Prepare for the W2 Form as an Employee

It is important to receive your W-2 from your employer annually in order to file your personal tax return. You have a role to play as an employee in keeping track of tax documents like W-2s. Use these tips to save W-2s and other important tax documents.

1. Keep important tax documents.

The W-2 shows your wage income and any amounts withheld from it for tax, Medicare, and Social Security. All of this information must be reported accurately on your tax returns. The W-2s you receive are used to support the amounts of income and taxes withheld that you declare.

Keep your tax return and any supporting documentation for up to seven years. W-2s and 1099s are included, as well as records of charitable contributions, mortgage interest statements, property tax records, or any other information related to taxes. Retaining past returns helps verify your income if it is ever audited.

Longer retention periods of 6-7 years may be advisable if:

- Your returns are complicated if you have assets such as businesses or investments.

- If you have made large donations to charity, they can be carried forward.

- If you claim bad debts or stock losses, they are not worth anything.

- If you have unresolved tax issues or pending legal cases, we can help.

- You may have a statute of limitations that is longer than the IRS standard limit.

2. Organize your tax records.

Store your tax documents, including W-2s, in a safe, secure location. You can also use safe deposit boxes or fireproof filing cabinets. Once the time limit has passed, you may wish to hire a shredding company to dispose of your records.

Sort records by type and year. Keep all materials that are needed to support the tax returns for each year together. You could use simple folders arranged by year. Use an electronic document management system on your computer or in the cloud. Just make sure that records can be easily accessed if necessary.

3. Keep original physical copies.

Keep original copies, such as your W-2s. The IRS may not accept photocopies or scanned versions as proof. As an additional form of identification, try to keep the original W-2s that show your name and address.

Official electronic versions provided to you by your employer or financial institution can be considered original documents. A PDF copy of your W-2 that you downloaded through your employer's website is original. Download and save your W-2 as soon as possible.

4. Reprints are available upon request.

Request a duplicate W-2 from your employer if you have lost the original. Employees are entitled to duplicate W-2s. A reasonable charge may apply for more than two copies per year.

Be aware that identity verification may be required to ensure the protection of your personal data when you request a W-2 replacement. To confirm your identity, provide information such as your Social Security number.

5. Change your address with the employer.

Notify your employer if you change addresses during the course of the year. You can be sure that your W-2 is mailed correctly. Even after you leave the company, notify them so that your last annual W-2 is sent to you.

You can usually update your address easily via the online HR/Payroll portal of your employer. If you prefer, notify the office in writing. It is also helpful to have the current details of your contact on record in case you need replacements.

6. Check Before Filing Your Return

Check your W-2 carefully before you file your taxes. Verify that the information regarding your employer, including its name, contact details, ID number, and address, is accurate. Check that your Social Security number, name, wage earned, and tax withheld match the records you have.

Compare the total of Medicare, Social Security, and federal tax withheld against your paystub. Inform your employer of any errors or omissions on the W-2 so that they may be rectified or modified before filing taxes. You can save yourself a lot of headaches by ensuring that your W-2 is correct.

7. Filing accurate returns on time

Use your W-2 to file an accurate and complete personal tax return each year by the IRS deadline, which is typically April 15th. Verify that you have reported the income on your W-2 and any other relevant documents. Calculate your deductions and credits correctly. If you fail to include certain W-2 earnings, penalties and interest can be charged for unpaid tax.

Pay your taxes on time to prevent penalties and interest. To receive your refund sooner, you should file as soon as possible. If you notice that refunds are taking longer than normal to process, follow up. Send the IRS any additional information they request as soon as possible.

8. Protection of sensitive data

Protect your personal data on documents such as your W-2. Forms should be kept in a secure place, and unneeded copies should be shredded. Avoid phishing emails that request your personal information. IRS never initiates contact via email, SMS, or other social media.

Share sensitive data, such as your social security number, credit card number, or bank account details, only through verified and secure platforms. Be alert for signs of identity theft and report any concerns immediately to the IRS.

Common Questions and Concerns of Employees

Many employees still have questions about the W-2 form, even if they've completed their preparation checklist and gathered all the necessary documents.

Here is a list of common questions, scenarios, and advice on how to proceed:

What happens if I change my marital situation? Verify that all HR documentation has been updated. It is important to update all HR paperwork.

Can I merge my W-2s if I have two jobs? You must report all sources of income accurately and file each W-2 individually.

How do I proceed if one or both of my W-2s are missing? To file your W-2 on time, request a copy of Form 4852 and substitute accurate estimates in place of it.

How do I get my W-2 if the former employer refuses to give it to me? Even after the filing season, you can still get your missing W-2 by using Form 4852. (Read more on this later in the book.)

When reporting my self-employment income, is it different? Your W-2 wage from your employer is still reported as normal. The self-employment income is reported separately.

Ask a professional tax advisor if you have any questions about how to handle complex or multiple W-2s based on the unique circumstances of your situation.

Ways You Can Identify Mistakes and Errors As An Employee

Even though most employees get accurate W-2s, errors do happen. There are a few clues to look for that indicate an incorrect Form W-2.

- The employer's name or address is incorrect.

- The employee's name, SSN, or contact information does not match.

- The compensation amounts appear to be significantly deflated or inflated.

- The tax withholding amount is drastically different.

- You may have state taxes deducted even if you do not live in the state.

- Where data should be present, blanks are displayed, or the reverse.

By carefully reviewing all entries, you can identify any anomalies, errors, and missing data. To resolve any errors before filing taxes, employees should immediately contact their employer's HR/payroll team. If you don't correct errors, it can cause delays and other problems.

What issues should be reported to the IRS

The IRS will need to intervene in some cases if employers fail to provide correct W-2s despite reasonable attempts, such as:

- W-2 refusal to be issued by the employer

- Significant efforts do not produce a corrected W-2.

- The employer is not available or cooperative.

- Fraud is suspected in the inaccurate reporting.

If you report such cases to the IRS using Form 4852 and provide as much documentation as possible, it can ignite a fire that will increase pressure on employers who refuse to comply and do not properly declare wages or give W-2s to their employees.

What impact could W-2 issues have on tax refunds and filing

Even if you try to anticipate any issues, W-2 problems can cause delays in tax refunds or require that amended returns be filed.

- IRS questions and flags about missing or incorrect data on the W-2

- The processing and approval of refunds may be delayed.

- The filing deadline is rapidly approaching, forcing alternative filings.

- You may need to amend your tax return later after receiving corrected W-2 forms.

- W-2s that are inaccurate continue to be a source of dispute between employees and employers.

Although major problems are unlikely if errors are discovered early on, refund-seeking employees are more sensitive to any delays in identifying or correcting W-2 mistakes after the tax season has begun. A quick response increases the likelihood of a smooth tax filing process and a speedy refund.

How to avoid common W-2 issues

There are simple things that employees can do to prevent many W-2 problems.

- Confirm details and provide up-to-date contact information with your employer.

- Check each pay stub and payroll site as you go for accuracy.

- Keep pay stubs for comparison with W-2s later.

- Be on the lookout for mistakes in marital status or exemptions.

- Ask about W-2 delivery methods and timing well in advance.

- If you do not receive your W-2s by January, please request replacements.

- Keep a cordial relationship with your manager and HR in the event of any issues later.

Even minor errors can be caught quickly, and if you are assured that things will be handled correctly from the beginning, it helps to prevent or resolve future mistakes.

Get professional assistance with your W-2 issues.

It is hoped that being proactive will result in a W-2 experience free of issues every year. Even seasoned workers may encounter issues that require professional help.

Unresolved Issues: If you are unable to resolve errors, tax professionals can contact HR/Payroll at your employer directly and fix the mistakes. They may also file Form 4852 in your name if all other attempts have failed. If corrections are made after the filing season, they can prepare revised returns.

Complex Issues: Expertise is required to resolve complex issues. Line-item discrepancies of a large magnitude, multiple W-2s, or the involvement of several employers can require expert assistance.

Second opinion: This can be helpful if something seems a little off about your W-2. An outside expert may provide some reassurance or even catch subtle issues before you file.

Tax planning for the end of the year: A professional can help you adjust your W-4 withholdings based on changes in marital status or other factors such as income, deductibility, and exemptions.

Accounting and tax professionals have the resources, expertise, contacts, and services to help employees navigate through even tricky W-2 issues or give them filing advice.

Chapter 5

The Standard Deduction and Itemized Tax Deductions.

Now that we understand the W-2 form and how to properly prepare for it, we can now focus on saving money by reducing our taxes. Deductions are a great way for employees to reduce their tax liability and taxable earnings. These amounts can be deducted from gross wages in order to determine your taxable final income. The tax code offers two options for deductions: the standard deduction and itemizing deductions.

This chapter will examine these choices of deduction in depth. We'll discuss the meaning of the standard deduction, how to claim itemized deductions, as well as tax-saving tips. The right strategy for deductions tailored to suit your financial situation will help you maximize your tax breaks and retain more of what you earn.

This chapter may reveal new opportunities for deductions, whether you use the standard method or list a lot of expenses. The key to minimizing your tax burden is optimizing deductions. Understanding deductions, along with handling the W-2 correctly, gives employees another tool to help them control their tax situation every year.

You have two main options to lower your tax liability: itemize or take the standard deduction. The standard deduction is the choice of most taxpayers because it requires less effort than itemizing. However, it may not be the best option for all. This chapter will explore it in more detail.

Understanding deductions when it comes time to file your taxes is crucial to maximizing your refund potential or minimizing what you owe. A deduction is a sum you can deduct from your income tax to lower the total amount that will be subjected to taxes.

Simple math can tell you the difference between itemized and standard deductions. Standard deductions lower your income by a fixed amount. The itemized deductions, on the other hand, are a collection of expenses that qualify. The deduction that reduces the tax you owe most can be claimed. Both are prohibited.

Standard Deduction

Standard deductions are dollar amounts that you can subtract from your gross adjusted income by the IRS to reduce the income tax you pay. The amount of the standard deduction that you are entitled to depends on whether or not you file taxes.

Those who are blind or 65 years old or older get an increased standard deduction. If you are dependent on someone else, your standard deduction may be lower.

The IRS allows most taxpayers to take the standard tax deduction without asking any questions, even if they have no other deductions or credits that qualify. Some taxpayers may not be eligible to take the standard deduction.

An example of a standard deductibility A married couple with taxable income of $125,000 and an adjusted gross income of $125,000 can claim a deduction of $27700. The tax deduction reduces the couple's taxable income from $125,000 to $97,000 ($125,000–$27,700).

How Does the Standard Deduction Work?

Either you can itemize your taxes or take the standard tax deduction. Standard deductions are a guaranteed, blanket amount that you can deduct from your AGI. You do not have to provide any proof to the IRS. The itemized deductions reduce taxable income, but they do so in a slightly different manner.

The IRS allows you to reduce your income by itemizing deductions. Some of these expenses include property taxes, unreimbursed health care costs, and business mileage.

If you choose the standard deduction, then certain tax benefits and mortgage interest cannot be deducted. Keep all records if you choose to itemize your deductions in case the IRS conducts an audit of you.

When can you not take the standard deduction?

Standard deductions are welcome for many, but in some cases, you might not qualify.

- Your spouse files separately and chooses itemization. Then you must itemize.

- If you are filing as a partnership, trust, or estate, please select the appropriate option.

- Due to accounting changes, your return may cover a shorter period than one year.

- If you are a dual-status or nonresident alien of the U.S., then your status is considered "nonresident.".

Standard deduction 2023 (taxes due April 2024)

For 2023, the standard deduction for married couples filing jointly and separately was $27,700, while for heads of households, it was $20,800.

Filing Status	2023 Standard Deduction
For single or married filing separately	$13,850
For married filing jointly or qualifying widow(er)	$27,700
For head of household	$20,800

Blind people and those older than 65 have higher standard deductions.

Standard Deduction 2024

Standard deductions for 2024 are $14,600 for those filing as singles or married filers separately. Joint filers can claim $29,200, while heads of households get $21,900. Tax returns for 2025 will claim the standard deduction of 2024.

Filing status	2023 standard deduction
For single or married filing separately	$14,600
For married filing jointly or qualifying widow(er)	$29,200
For head of household	$21,900

Standard deduction for dependents

You will have a standard deduction if you file a tax return. For the year, you can either choose a flat $1250 deduction or to deduct your entire earned income plus an additional $400. If you select the second option, your standard deduction cannot be exceeded.

For the year 2024 the standard deductibility for dependents is increased to $1300, equal to the earned income plus 400, without exceeding the maximum standard deduction.

Who can you claim as a tax dependent?

Tax purposes distinguish between two types of dependents.

- Qualifying child
- Qualifying Relative

Who is a Qualifying Child?

To be eligible to claim your child as a dependent on the tax return, it must meet all of these conditions.

1. Your child must be a part of the family

Relationship test: The child must be yours, a foster or adopted child of yours, a brother, sister, 'half-brother/half-sister, stepbrother/stepsister, or descendant from any of these people.

2. You must be below a certain age

This is an age-test. The following conditions must be met to pass this test:

1. The child cannot be older than you. If the child turns 18 before the end of the calendar year, they are eligible.

2. The child, if you're married and filing jointly with your spouse (and the child is under 23 at the end of the year), must also be younger. Student should have also been younger. The child must have been in college full time for at least five months of the year.

3. The child may be permanently disabled, even if the doctor determines that they have reached their limits.

3. The child has to live with you

It is easy to pass the residency test. The child must have lived with you for more than half of the calendar year. The year includes children who were born, died, or in juvenile detention.

In most cases, the parent with custody is entitled to claim their child as a dependent. Children can be claimed as dependents by noncustodial parent. It is usually necessary for the parent with custody to sign a statement that they won't claim their child as a dependent.

4. Children who are unable to meet more than half of their own financial needs

If your child has a job and provides at least half of his or her financial support, you cannot claim them as a dependent. However, support includes household expenses such as food, utilities, and clothing. The program also includes unreimbursed medical expenses, travel and recreation costs, etc.

5. The child cannot file jointly with another person.

This is because the joint tax return serves as a test. The exception is applicable if the spouse and child file a joint return in order to get a refund of income tax withheld or estimated tax paid.

6. The child must have a citizenship or a status of residency.

This test determines whether the child has a US passport, is an American resident alien, or is US-national. The child has to be a U.S. citizen, U.S. resident alien, U.S. national, or a Canadian, Mexican, or Canada-based resident. Adopted children are exempt from this rule.

Who is a Qualifying Relative?

The relative can be any age. For your relative to be claimed as your dependent on your tax return, they have to meet all conditions.

1. The child cannot be the eligible child of another person

You cannot claim the child as your qualifying relative if they are not a qualifying child. You cannot claim your toddler as a qualified relative if, for example, he or she lives with you and is eligible to be their child.

2. The person must be a family member or live with you.

Two statements are true.

- You are related in at least one of the following: they could be your niece, nephew, sibling or half-sibling or stepsibling (including kids from your half siblings). They could also be your nephew or niece, or your sibling, half-sibling, or stepsibling.

- The person you lived with all of the year can be excluded. You can exclude children who are divorced or separated, or have been abducted.

You can only pass the test if you meet one of the two requirements. You don't need to live with your relative in order to receive a credit. This is particularly useful to those supporting elderly parents who live elsewhere.

3. The threshold is the income of the individual.

The maximum annual gross income that an individual can earn in 2022 is $4400. In 2023, the tax due for 2024 will increase by $4700. Exemptions are available for disabled people with income from covered workshops. Gross income includes rental incomes and business profits as well as unemployment benefits, Social Security, and other payments.

4. A person receiving financial assistance must get more than half of their total income.

Support includes, in general, expenses such as rent, clothing, utilities, meals, and medical expenses that aren't reimbursed. It also includes travel costs, recreational costs, and non-reimbursed medical expenses. Multiple Support Declaration: When more than one individual provides financial support for a single person but that no person is able to provide 50% or more of the support, the declaration of multiple support allows those who are providing support to choose which person they want to claim as their tax dependent.

Who Doesn't Count as A Tax Dependent?

Tax dependents are not generally considered to be the following individuals.

- If someone can claim you, then anyone can.

- In general, couples who file joint returns are considered to be one unit. There are some important exceptions.

- Anyone who is not a U.S. citizen, U.S. resident alien, U.S. national, or a resident of Canada or Mexico (there are exceptions here for people adopting children).

- People hired to do work for you.

- Foreign students.

Tax Credits and Deductions Available for Dependents

- **Earned Income Tax Credit:** The earned income tax credit is the most important financial assistance program for people who are working and have a low or moderate income. This refundable credit reduces income taxes and increases tax refunds. It can be as high as $7,430 per family of three children or more in 2023. The amount will increase to $7.830 in 2024. The credit is not dependent on having children. However, the amount of the credit will be higher for taxpayers with qualifying children.

- **Credit for child and dependent care:** The refundable credit is designed to help parents cover the cost of daycare when a dependent qualifies for it, whether they are working or going to school. This credit is between 20 and 50 percent of eligible expenses up to $6,000.

- **Additional Child Tax Credit and Child Tax Credit**

  - Child tax credits are up to $2000 per child who qualifies and is under the age of 17.

  - The Child Tax Credit will be $3,600 in 2021 for every qualifying child aged 6–17 years old and $3,000 for children under 6 years of age. The American Rescue Plan brought about these new changes. They are available to single or separate married filers who earn up to $75,000. Joint filers can earn up to $150,000. You can still get the $2,000 additional credit per child if you exceed these thresholds. This is calculated using your original child tax credit income and phase-out amounts. The entire child tax credit will be fully refundable in 2021.

- **Credits for dependents other than your own:** You can claim up to $500 in non-refundable credits if you list a relative who qualifies as a dependent on the return. This credit can be claimed for every qualifying relative listed on your return.

- **Credit for adoption:** In 2023, the tax credit covers up to $16,950 in expenses that you have paid towards adoption. The credit will increase to $16,810 in 2024. The credit is not refundable, but you can carry forward any unused value for up to 5 years. How much adoption expense you have relates to the amount of credit that you are eligible for. If you spend $7,000 on adoption in 2023, you cannot claim the entire $15,950 credit. If you have $20,000 worth of adoption costs, your credit is limited to $15,950.

- **American Opportunity Tax Credit (AOC) and Lifetime Education Credit (LEC):** Both of these tax credits cover a portion of qualified educational expenses. You, your spouse, or any dependents can qualify for this credit if they are enrolled in college, vocational training, or work-related education.

- **Medical expenses.** You may deduct medical expenses paid by you or your child, relative, or dependent. However, there are rules that apply to the medical expense deduction. This means that you are able to deduct any unreimbursed qualified medical expenses above 7.5% of adjusted gross income. This deduction requires that you itemize all of your expenses on Schedule A. You can no longer claim the standard tax deduction.

Standard Deductions and Their Advantages

The standard deduction is a dollar-for-dollar reduction in your adjusted gross income. Standard deductions are a dollar-for-dollar reduction in your gross adjusted income.

Many people prefer to itemize their tax returns than take advantage of the standard deduction.

- Standard deductions are faster. Standard deductions make tax preparation relatively easy. It may be for this reason that most people choose to use the standard deduction instead.

- Every year, the standard deduction is adjusted to reflect inflation.

- Depending on their age, some people get more and others less. The standard deductions for people 65 and older as well as those who are blind, is higher. The filing status is still important. Your standard deduction will be smaller if someone declares you to be their dependent.

- Note to married couples. If you're married but filing separately, and your spouse is requesting itemized deductions, the standard deduction will not be available. You and your spouse both must choose the same option - standard deduction or itemized deductions.

What is an Itemized Deduction?

Itemized deductions are a way to reduce your AGI, but they do so in a slightly different manner than standard deductibility. As its name implies, the standard deduction is a fixed amount. Itemized deductions, however, are dollar-for-dollar and vary from taxpayer to taxpayer. Subtract the sum of all your deductions from your total income. These are some common itemized deductions.

There are different types of itemized tax deductions.

Itemized deductions can be complicated. Each type of itemized deduction has its own rules. You should understand their benefits and decide if it makes sense for you.

Here are some examples of common itemized deductions.

1. Medical Expenses

The taxpayer can subtract from their income the percentage of unreimbursed medical and dental expenses they have accrued over the past year. The key term is unreimbursed: only expenses paid by the taxpayer are eligible. It means that your insurance will not cover or reimburse these expenses. These can include prescription drugs, payments to doctors, hospitalization, and dentures, among other costs.

The Rules for Medical Expense Tax Deductions

The key rules for deducting medical costs from your tax return are:

- You must list your medical expenses on Schedule A when filing your federal tax return. This deduction is not available to taxpayers who claim the standard deduction.

- Only medical expenses that exceed 7.5% of your gross adjusted income are deductible. You must meet this threshold before you can deduct anything.

- The qualified expenses are payments for medical costs, such as doctors' fees, dental care, vision services, hospitalization, prescription drugs, insurance premiums, and transportation related to healthcare, along with lodging costs, long-term services, or other approved expenses.

- Cosmetic procedures or treatments that are unnecessary and/or cosmetic do not usually qualify for medical deductions. Expenses must be used primarily to alleviate or prevent a mental or physical defect.

- You, your spouse, or any dependents who are capable of covering medical costs can make payments for medical expenses. However, neither an insurance provider nor any other sources can reimburse them.

- The deduction is available to all taxpayers, regardless of age or income. The deduction is applicable from the moment of birth until death, provided that expenses are above the AGI threshold.

2. Property tax deduction

State and Local Taxes (SALT) allows homeowners who pay high property tax amounts to deduct up to $10,000 in local, state, and federal taxes. If you're married but filing separately, your deduction will be capped at $5,000.

What property is tax-deductible?

- Apartments co-op

- Primary home

- Vacation homes.

- Land.

- Purchase property outside of the United States.

- Vehicles such as cars, RVs, and others.

- Boats.

What doesn't count as a property tax deduction?

Property tax is not deductible by the IRS for:

- Taxes on real estate that you do not own

- You haven't yet paid your property taxes.

- Assessments for the construction of streets, sidewalks, or sewer and water systems within your community. Assessments or taxes paid for the maintenance and repair of these things can be deducted.

- Water or garbage, for instance.

- Taxes on the transfer of property.

- Assessments by homeowner associations

- For a combination property tax, state and local sales and income taxes (or both) that exceed $10,000 ($5,000 for married filers filing separately),.

The Rules for Property Tax Deduction

These are the main rules to follow when claiming an exemption for property taxes:

- Only real property that you personally own can be deducted. Included in this is your main residence as well as any other homes you own or invest in.

- Property tax is based on the value of the home. Included in this are the annual tax bills you receive from local and state tax authorities.

- Property taxes do not include special assessments by your local government, such as new sidewalks and sewers.

- State and local property tax can be deducted as an itemized deduction in Schedule A or as a standard deduction of up to $10,000 along with state income tax. The $10,000 limit applies to both married and single filers.

- Property taxes cannot be deducted on property that is rented out. Rental property expenses can instead be claimed for the property tax portion that is applicable to rentals.

- You can claim a deduction for the part of your property tax that is applicable to space you use exclusively and regularly as a business.

- The property tax must be paid in the calendar year in which you claim the deduction. According to local or state law, the amount also has to be assessed during that year.

3. Mortgage interest deduction

The itemized deduction is a way for taxpayers who have a mortgage and pay interest to reduce their income tax each year. The deduction is only available for up to $750,000 of mortgage debt. This applies whether the home you are using is your primary residence or a secondary one. For married couples filing separate returns, the maximum amount of mortgage interest that can be deducted is $375,000. There are different rules for mortgages obtained before December 2017.

What qualifies as mortgage interest?

The IRS's general definition of "mortgage interest" is interest that accrues from any loan secured by your primary home or second home. There are other costs and fees that can be included when claiming mortgage interest on taxes, too. This is a quick guide:

- Interest on your mortgage: the collateralized property has to include sleeping, eating, and cooking facilities. It can be a house, mobile home, or boat.

- You can deduct interest on the second home that you own, but don't let it go. Read up on the other tax deductions that you can claim for your rental property.

- You can deduct late payment fees.

- You can claim a deduction for prepayment penalties.

- You can claim a deduction for a percentage of the points you have paid to reduce your mortgage rate.

- You can claim interest on home equity loans or lines of credit that you use to renovate your house.

What costs of a mortgage are not tax deductible?

Some mortgage expenses aren't deductible with interest. Some of these costs include:

- Mortgage interest on a home that is a 3rd+

- You will not pay any interest until the reverse mortgage is paid.

- Payments for mortgage insurance

- Insurance for homeowners

- Appraisal fees

- Notary fees

- Close-out costs or down payment money

- Additional payments to the principal

- The interest on funds borrowed from your HELOC or home equity loan for non-property-related purposes (for instance, borrowing against your house in order to buy a vehicle or start a new business) is not deductible.

Rules for Mortgage Interest Deduction

The key rules for the deduction of mortgage interest are:

- You can deduct the interest on mortgages up to $750,000 if you use them to buy, construct, or renovate your main home and any designated second home. The mortgage interest deduction includes debt refinanced through a new loan.

- The interest paid on lines of credit or home equity loans is only deductible if it was used to purchase, construct, or substantially improve the property that secured the loan. The interest paid on home equity loans or lines of credit is only deductible if the funds are used to buy, build, or substantially improve the property that secures it.

- You must list your deductions in Schedule A on your federal income tax return to claim this deduction. This deduction is not available to those who claim the standard deduction.

- On your return, you must include the mortgage holder's name, address, and taxpayer ID number. Mortgage holders who held their mortgages before 2009 are granted an exception.

- The $750,000 limit on loans and the deduction are available to married couples who file jointly as well as single filers. The maximum qualifying debt for married single taxpayers filing separately but who are also married is $375,000.

- Before the deduction limit is phased out, investment properties and vacation properties must meet a lower threshold of $750,000/$375,000 for total mortgage debt across all properties owned.

4. Charitable contribution deduction

You can deduct donations made to IRS-recognized charities. Deductions are based on the type of contribution made. It is usually between 20 and 60%.

Remember the limitations and rules that apply:

- Dentist and medical costs. You can only deduct expenses that exceed 7.5% of your adjusted gross income in 2022.

- Local taxes include property taxes, income taxes, and state taxes. The TCJA limits the deductions for local and state taxes to $10,000. Prior to the TCJA, deductions for state and local taxes were unlimited.

- Mortgage interest. If you bought your home before December 16, 2017, then you can deduct interest on mortgages of up to $1,000,000. If you purchased your home after December 16, 2017, interest can be deducted up to $750,000. To qualify, the mortgage must have been used to "buy, build, or substantially improve" the house. The home equity loan that was not used for renovations or remodeling your house is not eligible.

- Tax deductions for donations to charity Donations go to charities.

- Theft and accidents are losses. Tax deductions are made for federally declared disasters.

If you have been itemizing for some time, it's possible that certain deductions have been removed from your list. Recent tax reforms have eliminated some miscellaneous itemized deductions. Included are investment fees, taxes, and job costs. Businesses can continue to deduct these expenses. The change only affected individual tax returns.

Benefits of Itemized Deductions

The following are the benefits of itemizing your deductions rather than taking the standard deduction when filing your tax return:

1. **It usually results in lower taxable revenue and tax liability**: For those who have deductible expenses such as mortgage interest, taxes, and charitable contributions that exceed the standard deduction, itemizing allows them to deduct more and lower their taxable income.

2. **Rewards for charitable contributions:** The standard deduction does not include a charitable deduction. You can reduce your taxes by itemizing gifts made to charitable organizations that qualify. This encourages donations.

3. **Homeownership is rewarded:** Itemizers are able to deduct the full amount of mortgage interest and property tax. If you itemize your deductions, buying a house with a mortgage will lower your tax bill.

4. **Encourages investment expenses:** Certain investment costs, such as investment interest and adviser fees, can be deducted from Schedule A under miscellaneous deductions.

5. Deductible state and local taxes in full: Prior to 2018, there was no limit on the deduction of state or local property and income taxes. Tax filers who live in areas with high taxes can lower their federal taxes by using an itemized approach.

6. Flexibility of timing deductions: With an itemized strategy, you can accelerate or delay expenses in order to maximize your tax savings.

Disadvantages of itemizing deductions

1. Knowing the rules is essential.

There are a few hurdles to itemized deductions. Only medical expenses that are greater than 7.5% can be deducted.

2. Require more time for your tax return.

If you choose to itemize, it may require more time for your tax return. Set aside extra time to complete Schedule A and Form 1040 and any accompanying schedules.

3. You must provide proof to support your deductions

You must keep track of your records and be organized. It means keeping your documents and being organized. If you plan to itemize next year, start saving your receipts.

Calculating your tax savings

The deductions you can make for itemized taxes are an excellent way to reduce your tax bill and lower your income. What tax bracket are you in?

Consider that you're a single tax payer, and you made $100,000 of taxable income in the last year. You are now in the 24% tax bracket.

You will have an income tax of $80,000 if you list your deductions. This puts you in the 22% bracket.

Your tax rate is still 24%, even if you only claim $10,000 in deductions.

Standard Deductions Vs Itemized Deductions

If your standard tax deductions are higher, you should use the amount that is allowed as a standard deduction. It's the same for the opposite.

To decide whether it's worth it, you will also have to know how much money you make and the itemized costs you intend to incur this year. Look at your last tax return.

Let's take Mark and Sara as an example. They are unsure if they will itemize deductions for 2023. They expect their 2023 income and deductions to be the same as in 2022. They take their 2022 Form 1040 and look at Line 7, which shows that their gross adjusted earnings were $100,000.

If we take a look at this list, Mark and Sara could be eligible for itemized deductions by 2023.

Dental and medical expenses

In order to be eligible for itemized health expenses, your medical and dental expenditures must exceed 7.5% of your AGI in 2023.

Mark and Sara must spend at least $7500 in medical expenses to qualify for a deduction. Mark and Sara have health insurance and are in good shape. Mark and Sara don't expect to undergo major medical or dental procedures by 2023. They do not anticipate medical costs exceeding $7500.

Medical expense itemized: $0

Local and state taxes

Mark makes estimated tax payments of $5,000 per quarter. Sara stays at home to care for her daughter, and so she does not pay any estimated taxes.

Mark and Sara each pay around $5,000 per year in property taxes on their home and $200 in personal property taxes with their vehicle registration. Mark and Sara can claim up to $10,000 in state and local taxes, or $10,200. Mark and Sara cannot claim an additional $200 because the state and local tax deductions are capped at $10,000.

The tax itemized is: $10,000.

The Interest Rate on a Mortgage

Mark and Sara pay about $8,000 per year in mortgage interest on their house. Mark and Sara have a mortgage of less than $750,000 and bought their home with all their proceeds.

The mortgage interest itemized: $8,000.

Give to charity.

Mark and Sara donate approximately 600 dollars each year in cash and 300 dollars of clothes, household items, and other used items to charity thrift stores.

Itemized charitable donations: $900

Calculate the total of your itemized deductions.

Mark and Sara expect their itemized deductions for 2023 to be around $18,900 ($10,000 in taxes, $8,000 in mortgage interest, and $900 on gifts). In 2023, the standard deduction will be $25,900 for married couples filing jointly. The itemized deductions of the married couple are therefore $700 lower than the standard deduction. Mark and Sara can claim the standard deduction for 2023, unless they intend to increase charitable donations or pay medical expenses.

You'll want to make sure you keep track of any itemized tax deductions that you may have, just in case. Your tax pro can compare the two methods to determine which one results in a lower tax liability.

Chapter 6

Tax-Advantaged Accounts and Contributions

Tax-advantaged savings accounts, such as 401(k), IRAs, HSAs, and FSAs are a great way to put money aside to pay for medical and retirement expenses. They come with restrictions on contribution amounts and have certain limitations, but they offer tax advantages that allow people to invest and save more easily than a standard investment account.

This chapter provides an overview of the tax-advantaged account types most commonly used by families and individuals. The chapter will cover key rules about eligibility, contributions, tax treatment, and withdrawals. Accounts covered include:

- 401(k) Plans

- Traditional IRAs

- Health Savings Accounts

- Flexible spending accounts

By understanding the pros and cons, people can develop better strategies for financial planning and management, retirement savings and health care. Even small decisions can have a significant impact in the long term.

What Is Tax-Advantage

Tax Advantage refers to an investment plan or savings plan that offers tax advantages such as tax deferral, tax exemption and tax reduction. Tax advantage includes government bonds, annuities, retirement plans, and any other investment plan that is authorized by the Tax Department of the country.

Investors can enjoy certain tax advantages by investing in tax-advantaged account types, like 401(k), IRAs, and so on. These all offer some form of tax benefit. These accounts allow you to contribute before tax or withdraw from them without tax. These accounts are loaded with benefits, but they come with conditions.

- Contribution limits

- Early withdrawal penalties

A traditional IRA, for example, allows you to make contributions before taxes are applied, reducing your taxable income. Tax-deferred investments mature in this account, so you don't have to pay taxes until after retirement. Although there are some limitations to the benefits, you still receive a substantial benefit. The more you keep these accounts open, the greater your benefits will be.

Importance of Tax Advantage

Encourages Investments. Proper investments using tax-advantaged funds will not only provide benefits for taxes but also promote investment strategies for individuals.

1. **Multi-Strategies:** Depending on an individual's financial situation and goals, there are several strategies available for tax-benefit accounts. The individual can choose which strategy is best for him or her.

2. **Future planning:** The individual plans his investment in the future, for example, retirement, education of children, health care, and wealth. These accounts give an overview of the market and can help determine which strategies each individual should use.

3. **Reducing Tax Burden:** With a variety of strategies, including tax-deferred and after-tax investment options, these investments can help you reduce your tax burden. For example, government bonds.

Types of Tax Advantage Accounts

1. **Pre-Tax Investment Accounts (Deferred Tax):** This investment will delay taxes until a future date, when the investments produce gains.

2. **After-Tax Investment Accounts:** Your tax already paid is credited to the account. These accounts do not charge taxes on gains or earnings up to certain limits.

Pre-Tax Accounts

The U.S. uses 401(k), 457(b), and 403(b) as employer-sponsored savings plans. Most of these plans have an employee funding them, but certain employers match the contributions.

1. 401(k):

The 401(k), or employer-sponsored retirement account, is one of the largest and most common types of accounts for saving money in the United States. Employees can make pre-tax payments from their pay, which lowers their current taxable income while putting money aside for retirement. This will grow tax-deferred with time. There are certain rules that apply to withdrawals and contributions.

The employer is responsible for sponsoring a defined contribution retirement plan. The employee can deduct a certain percentage from each pay check from their 401(k). This is done on a pretax basis. The employee can lower their taxable income while saving for retirement.

Funds contributed to a retirement plan are typically invested in a mixture of mutual funds, stocks, and bonds. Taxes are deferred based on the growth of the investment or the earnings that are generated.

If an employee withdraws money in retirement and pays income taxes, the tax is based on his or her income tax rates at that point. While no tax is paid on earnings or contributions over time, withdrawals from retirement accounts are subject to income taxes.

Contribution limits for 401(k)

The 401(k), by allowing employees to make pre-tax payments, helps them lower their current taxable income while also saving money for the future. The government limits the amount employees can deposit into these accounts every year.

The employee contribution cap for 2023 is $22,500. This applies to those who are under 50 years old. The catch-up contribution for employees over 50 years old is up to $7500. Over 50s can make a total contribution of up to $30,000.

These limits only apply to elective deferrals made by employees. Employer matching funds are not included in the limits if an employer matches an employee's contributions from his or her salary to a 401(k).

If an employee exceeds the limit, they must refund excess contributions or face penalties and taxes. IRS may increase the 401(k) contribution limits over time to reflect inflation and other economic factors.

Rules for 401(k) Withdrawals and Early Access

The 401(k), or retirement plan, is a great way to save for your future without paying taxes every year on capital gains and investment income. In exchange for the tax advantage, however, there are rules that govern when funds in 401(ks) can be accessed.

from The 401(k), or retirement, plans were designed to help provide savings and income after you leave the workplace and reach retirement age. In most situations, an IRS 10% penalty is applied to withdrawals from 401(k). Except in cases of death, disability, or separation from service after or during the year that the employee turns 55, the IRS applies a 10% early withdrawal penalty tax.

For early withdrawals, you will be charged a 10% fee in addition to paying income tax on the amount distributed. To avoid this, it is best to leave 401(k), or retirement funds, untouchable until the age of retirement unless you absolutely need them.

Once an employee has reached age 59 and 1/2, he or she can withdraw 401(k) funds, without any penalties. The IRS considers this age to be the standard retirement age when allowing penalty-free withdrawals from retirement accounts.

401(k) If you withdraw money at 59 1/2 years older more, it is considered income, and taxes are due. Once this age has been reached, there are no penalties for early withdrawals. Many retirees delay taking out their 401(k), beyond the age of 59 1/2 to take advantage of more tax-deferred earnings before converting to taxable income.

401(k)When changing jobs, it is important to know that existing 401(k), balances may be transferred into the plan of the new employer, moved to a non-profit IRA, or cashed in with penalties and taxes if you are under age 591/2. Most people choose to transfer their existing 401(k), or IRA, balances to a traditional IRA to keep the tax-deferred status up until retirement.

Additional Rules for 401(k) and Plan Considerations

Some other important aspects of 401(k) plans beyond the IRS contribution limitations and distribution rules that we have covered here include:

Matching contributions Many employers offer matching contributions for employee 401(k)s in order to encourage participation and save money for retirement. It is not uncommon for employers to match "100%" of the first 3 percent of a salary. If an employee pays 3% of their pay to a 401(k), then the employer will match that amount. The 401(k), when offered, can greatly increase retirement savings.

1. **Vesting Requirements**

401(k)Any matching funds provided by an employer with a 401 (k) plan will be subject to vesting requirements that dictate when these employer dollars are fully owned by the employee. The vesting schedule most commonly used is 20% vesting per year over a period of 5 years, until the employee has 100% ownership after 5 years. If an employee leaves a company before being fully vested, they will lose some or all of the employer match funds.

2. Investments and Fees

401(k) plans require you to choose from the investment options offered by the plan. The majority of plans provide a selection of stocks and bond mutual funds. Some plans offer target-date funds, which automatically change to a more conservative allocation as you approach retirement. In order to maintain a retirement savings account, plan administrators charge their employees fees. count. This can lower net returns.

3. Loans

Some 401(k) plans offer employees the opportunity to borrow from their savings, even while they are still employed. It allows employees to access funds they would not otherwise have until retirement. Loans can disrupt compound growth in the account, and they must be paid back. If you fail to pay back a loan from your 401(k), it becomes taxable and subject to penalties.

4. RMDs: Required Minimum Distributions.

Once a person reaches the age of 72, the IRS mandates that they begin to withdraw a certain amount each year from their tax-deferred account like a 401(k), traditional IRAs, and IRA plans based on calculations for life expectancy. The IRS requires these minimum distributions to prevent tax deferral indefinitely. If you fail to withdraw the required RMDs, a penalty equal to 50% of that amount will be charged.

2. 403(b)

The 403(b) plan is an account for retirement that's available to those who are employed in the public sector and by certain tax-exempt 501(c)(3) organizations. This is similar to the 401(k), which employers offer more frequently in the private sector. Government employees, doctors, librarians, and self-employed ministers are among the most common users of a 403(b).

A 403(b), like a 401k, allows you to save a part of every paycheck towards your retirement. Your employer can also match your contribution if they choose. Tax-deferred 403(b) accounts are those where your contributions lower your income tax this year, and then you pay tax on the distributions you receive in retirement. Roth 403(b) accounts, on the other hand, allow you to pay tax on contributions now and let your money grow tax-free later.

Participants should know about a few important components of 403(b).

- Limits on annual contributions: The total contribution limit for 2023 is $66,000 if you are under 50 years old or $73,000 if you're over 50.

- In most cases, withdrawals made before the age of 59 1/2 are subject to 10% penalties in addition.

- IRS regulations require that account holders begin to withdraw minimum amounts at 72 years old, based on their life expectancy.

- Employee vesting may be required for employer matching. This could require several years' employment to fully own the matches.

The rules regulate tax-advantaged retirement accounts to provide income for retirees. They are complex but offer substantial long-term savings.

What are the similarities between 401(k) and 403(b)?

The 403(b), like the 401(k), is similar. Both plans offer employees an opportunity to invest in retirement at a lower tax rate. The basic contribution limit is the same for both: $22,500 by 2023 and $23,000 by 2024.

Employee and employer contributions are limited to $66,000 ($69,000) in 2023 (or 100% of an employee's last yearly salary in 2024).

The Roth option is available in both plans. Participants must reach the age of 59 1/2 before they can withdraw their funds. The 403(b), like a 401k, offers catch-up contributions of $7500 for people 50 years of age and older. In 2024, the amount will remain unchanged.

What makes 403(b) a plan different from the 401(k)?

The 403(b), or retirement account, shares many similarities with the 401(k) plan. Some key differences are:

Employees of schools, hospitals, and religious institutions are eligible for 403(b). A 401(k) plan is available to employees in the private sector.

Contribution limits: In 2023, 403(b), plans may allow employee and employer combined contributions of up to $73,000 ($73,000. if you are over 50 years old). The 401(k) elective deferral limit is lower, at just $22,500. Employer contributions can be up to $66,000.

Roth Accounts: Roth accounts allow after-tax contributions, while traditional 401(ks) require pre-tax funds.

Investments: 403(b)s have a more restricted investment selection than 401(k), and they rarely include company stock.

The availability of 403(b), or loan provisions, varies much more in comparison to 401(k) plans.

Both types of plans offer similar tax benefits. The 403(b), however, is a non-profit plan, so there are differences in terms of eligibility, contribution amounts, and investment options.

Maximizing your 403(b).

Contributing diligently to a 403(b)-retirement plan over time can compound the savings of eligible employees. Contributing $300 per month over 30 years and earning an average return of 7% results in more than $650,000.

This is even faster if you maximize any matching funds from your employer. Investing early also allows for more compounded growth over time.

The 403(b), therefore, confers major advantages in retirement savings. Understanding the rules and maximizing the benefits requires understanding tax advantages, consistent contributions over time, prudent investing, and knowing the rules. These actions can lead to significant wealth accumulation that will provide security for retirement.

3. 457 Plan

The 457 plans, which is non-qualified and tax-advantaged and available for employees of local and state governments as well as certain tax-exempt organizations,

The 457 plan allows pre-tax contributions through payroll deferral. The assets are tax-deferred and can be used to increase retirement savings.

The 457 plan is a government-sponsored employer retirement account that confers certain benefits, but it also has limitations.

- Employees can elect to defer up to $22,500 in the 457 plan by 2023. There is a $7,500 catch-up for employees over 50.

- The total annual contribution allowed for 457 employees and employers is $25,000.

- The assets grow in value tax-deferred, and the distributions are taxed at the ordinary income rate.

- There is no early withdrawal penalty, allowing you to access the account at any time.

- Governments can restrict distribution for 90 days or more after a service member leaves.

This makes 457s an excellent tool to help public sector workers accumulate significant assets.

How do 457 plans work?

Employers can provide 457 accounts to eligible employees of state and local governments. These are similar to 401(k), but they give them the opportunity to contribute a portion of their paycheck.

The contribution limits in 2023 will allow you to defer 100% of your income, up to a maximum amount of $22,500 for those under 50 years old and $30,000. If using catch-up contributions at age 50 or older, The total contribution, including employer matches under 457, cannot exceed $25,000.

The money is invested in mutual funds that invest in stocks and bonds, with the hope of a long-term appreciation. Compound growth is possible because taxation has been deferred.

Contrary to 401(k), 457 plans allow access at any age, including before age 59 and 1/2. Although intended to be used for retirement, emergency withdrawals that are eligible and unforeseeable can provide access earlier if needed.

457 Distribution and Withdrawal Guidelines

The 457 account has a key advantage over the other plans in that there is no penalty for early withdrawals, regardless of your age. Nevertheless, there are still some guidelines for distribution:

- Only those who are under 72 years old and working can withdraw from their employment.

- Access is allowed upon separation, but certain employers require up to 90-day delays.

- Minimum distributions are required to avoid IRS penalties at 72 years old.

- Only in unforeseeable emergencies can hardship withdrawals be made.

While 457 plans allow for the most flexibility in terms of withdrawals, there are still some restrictions on distributions while you're working. This access provides income from early retirement to age 59 1/2 before a 401(k), IRA, or taxable IRA can be accessed.

Investment Options and Account Administration

The 457 plan allows participants to choose from a variety of investment options, including mutual funds that invest in stocks and bonds, as well as cash equivalents and funds for target-date retirement.

The government, as the plan sponsor, can manage plan administration, including compliance, records, statements, and other tasks, internally or hire external firms for these services. The administrative costs are passed on to participants either directly or via investment expense ratios.

Optional rollovers for 457 accounts

Upon leaving employment, the balance of a 457 plan can be rolled into another 457 sponsored by an employer, transferred into an IRA, or cashed in with tax owed. It could also potentially go into another qualified retirement plan.

By consolidating all 457 plans into one IRA, the required minimum distributions will begin at 72 years old. If assets are spread across multiple old plans, they may trigger several separate distribution streams.

Some employers in the government offer matching contributions to their 457 plans, for example, 50% of deferrals by employees up to 6% of salary. This is a 50 percent return on the contributions made up to this threshold.

Make sure you maximize the matching contribution offered every year. Compound growth allows these contributions to significantly increase retirement savings over time.

Compare the key features between 401(k), 403(b), and 457 retirement plans.

Eligibility

- Employed by state and local governments and tax-exempt organizations

- Employed by public schools, hospitals, and churches, as well as 501(c)(3) non-profits

- Employees of private companies can enroll in a 401(k).

Maximum Employee Contribution for 2023

- The standard contribution is $22,500, but you can get up to $30,000 if you're 50+.

- 403(b), standard contribution of $22,500, plus $30,000 if you are 50+.

- 401(k), standard contribution: $22,500, with a catch-up of $30,000 if you are 50+

Maximum Employer Contribution

- The combination of employee and employer is limited to $25,000.

- Contributions combined under 403(b), limited to $73,000 per annum for those aged 50+

- Combination contributions are limited to $73,000 per year for those aged 50+ or $66,000 per year for everyone else.

The Early Withdrawal Penalty
- There is no penalty for withdrawals at any time.

- If you withdraw your 401(k) or 403(b), there is a 10% penalty.

The funds are available.
- Some employers require 90 days after departure.

- 403(b), 401(k), age of 59 1/2, without penalty

Investing in the future
- All plans permit investing in stocks, bonds, and mutual funds.

All retirement vehicles offer the same tax-deferred compounding growth. Minor differences in access, eligibility, and contributions can create small variations in the rules. There are 457 plans that allow penalty-free entry before the age of 59 1/2.

Individual Retirement Plan:

Contributions from the individual are deductible. If an employer sponsors a plan for an employee and that individual's income exceeds the modified adjusted gross income limit, the contribution to the plan is not tax deductible.

The above-mentioned plans should be viewed from the perspective that, when an individual retires and takes their investment out, they are in the group with lower incomes compared to when they were employed, giving them tax advantages at a later date.

After-Tax Accounts:

After-tax contributions are money that is paid to a retirement account or an investment after the income tax on these earnings has been taken out. If you open a Roth or traditional retirement account with a tax advantage, the individual can choose whether to pay income taxes after retirement or defer them until retirement.

Some people, mainly those who earn more, can contribute their after-tax earnings to traditional accounts in addition to what is allowed before tax. The tax benefits are not immediate. Tax purposes require careful tracking of the money that is pre-taxed and after-tax.

Understanding after-tax contributions

The government provides several tax-favored retirement plans to encourage Americans to save for their future. These include the 401(k), which employers offer to employees. Also, anyone who has earned an income can access the IRA through a broker or bank.

The two options are available to most, but not everyone, who opens a retirement plan.

- Traditional retirement accounts allow their owners to invest "pre-taxed" money into an investment account. The money paid into the account is exempt from income taxes in the year of payment. Contributions reduce the saver's gross income tax for the year. When the account owner withdraws money from the account, which is likely to be after retirement, the IRS gets its share.

- Roth accounts are the option that is "after tax." The Roth account allows you to deposit money that has already been taxed. This is a bigger hit on the individual's take-home pay. After retirement, the balance of the account is not taxed again. Roth 401(k), also known as designated Roth options, is a newer option that not all employers offer. A certain amount of earnings is required to be able to contribute to a Roth IRA.

Tax savings plans

- ## Education tax-advantaged accounts

For public colleges, students borrow an average of $8000 per year, and for private colleges, they can borrow more than $9000. Start saving for an education savings account to assist a student in keeping their debt low.

Plan 529: College Savings

The 529 plan, which is similar to the Roth account, allows you to save for college tuition and other higher education expenses without paying taxes. You contribute your after-tax money, and the money will grow tax-free. Then, it can be spent tax-free, as long as money is used for tuition at college, student loans, or other expenses related to higher education.

One of the main distinctions between them is the fact that 529 plans are state-sponsored. You may be eligible for additional tax benefits in some states if you make a contribution.

You can transfer the funds to a family member or sibling if the person you were saving for doesn't need the full amount for college. This is better than withdrawing the money to use for anything other than school, as the beneficiary will have to pay 10% tax plus any gains.

Starting in 2024, beneficiaries will have the option to transfer money from this account at a lower cost. The 529 plan must have been established at least 15 years ago, and the money in the account needs to remain there for five years.

- **Coverdell Education Savings Account:**

A Coverdell Educational Savings Account (CESA) is a trust that allows you to set aside money for your child's future education. It's based on the Roth-style account: you contribute money after taxes, while earnings and withdrawals are qualified for tax exemptions. It can be used for either K–12 or college expenses.

The total contribution to each Coverdell ESA cannot exceed $2,000 per year. This account does not allow you to save as much money as many 529 plans. The ability to make contributions to Coverdell ESAs begins to diminish when you reach a modified AGI of $95,000 for single filers or $190,000.000 for joint filers.

- **Health Savings Accounts (HSA)**

In the U.S., healthcare costs **$4.3 billion** per year. Even if your insurance is good, expect to have to cover some of this out-of-pocket. In general, those with health insurance from their employers have to pay nearly $1,800 **a year** out of pocket before the insurance kicks in. Medicare may not be enough to cover the out-of-pocket health expenses of older adults in retirement.

It makes sense, therefore, to start saving early and set up a healthcare savings account. You can choose a tax-advantaged healthcare account to either prepare for future medical costs or set money aside for health expenses this year.

Chapter 7

Deductible Expenses for W2 Workers

As a W2 employee, you may be able to claim certain expenses as a deduction from your income tax when filing your annual return. These expenses need to be related to your job, and they must also be ordinary and needed. Taxable expenses lower your tax liability by reducing the amount you pay.

The most common expenses that W2 employees can deduct are unreimbursed expenses, deductions for home offices, travel expenses, uniforms and work clothes, costs of job searching, as well as expenses related to education and professional growth. The amount of deductions is limited and there are rules about what falls under each category. Documentation is required.

This section will give you an overview of all the types of expenses that are deductible for employees with W2, the requirements and what documents to keep. It also includes tips on how to maximize your deductions.

Unreimbursed Employee Expenses

Employee expenses that aren't reimbursed are costs incurred by you in connection with your work but not reimbursed by your employer. Some common examples include:

- Mileage incurred by your own vehicle for work-related purposes. Included are client meetings, travel to your office (if you work remotely) and trips between different locations. IRS standard mileage rates apply.

- You can claim travel expenses such as airfare, hotel costs, and up to 50% of the meal cost for work-related events like conferences or training seminars.

- You can buy your own work supplies, such as uniforms, books or journals, software for the job, etc.

- You will need to pay licensing and regulatory fees to keep your professional credential.

- Use your home and mobile internet for business purposes.

- If you are already working, job search costs include resume services, interviews and fees for placement firms.

You'll want to keep track of all the details, such as mileage, dates and locations. Also, make sure you have your receipts. Credit card statements are not enough documentation.

In addition, previously, expenses that were not reimbursed could only be deducted up to a maximum of 2% AGI. This deduction has been eliminated by the recent tax reform, which began in 2018. There are now greater restrictions but certain types of non-reimbursed costs may still qualify for a deduction.

Home Office Deduction

Most employees are now accustomed to working remotely or in hybrid arrangements, which require a dedicated home office. If you meet certain requirements, home office costs can be claimed on your taxes. You can deduct:

- Rent, mortgage interest and taxes, utility bills, internet, etc. are all included in the percentage. Based on your office's size in relation to your total home square footage.

- Renovations and repairs to your home specifically for the purpose of accommodating a home office.

- Exclusively for the home office, furniture and electronic devices.

- Remote work environments require special lighting, ergonomics, and equipment.

- Costs of home security systems and pest control for your office.

- The percentage of your condo/cooperative fees that is allocated to the home office.

You must be using the office space exclusively and regularly for your work to qualify for the deduction. This must also be the primary place where you do your work - administrative and management tasks. Also, meetings with customers, clients or patients count. Even if you use your laptop occasionally on the couch, it does not count.

You can claim a deduction up to $1,500 for the simplified option. This allows you to deduct $5 per sq. ft. of office space, up to a maximum of 300 square feet. The method allows you to avoid having to calculate exact percentages for home office costs.

Work-Related Travel Expenses

Tax deductions may be available for travel that you consider to be ordinary, necessary and directly connected with your work.

- Costs of transportation, including airfare, hotel, car rental, parking fees, tolls and other costs

- Baggage fees and travel charges

- Business travel expenses: 50% off

- If your trip exceeds one week, you may need to do some cleaning and laundry.

- Tipping service providers such as hotel porters and housekeepers or taxi drivers

- You will need to pay for Wi-fi or internet access in order to carry out your job duties while traveling

- Transport fees for equipment and shipment of samples

- Costs of communication services like business faxes and web conferences

- Business travel requires vaccinations and health precautions

Some types of commutes may qualify as well, for example traveling to an outside temporary job site from your usual daily commute. The trip expenses must directly relate to a business-related purpose and should not be considered vacation.

Work clothes and uniforms

If your employer requires it and the clothing is not appropriate for daily wear, you may be eligible to deduct these costs. You can, for example:

- On a building site, hard hats and safety goggles are required.

- Wearing steel-toed boots at a industrial facility

- Healthcare professionals wear scrubs and lab coats.

- Firefighters must wear flame retardant clothing

- Reservist military uniforms

- Commercial fishermen's foul weather gear

- Highway workers should wear reflective vests when constructing roads.

Business attire which could be worn as casual clothing is not acceptable, even when required by the employer. Suits, dress shirts and ties, dress boots, nylons or conventional shoes are examples.

Include the costs of cleaning and maintenance in your claim for work clothes. Add alterations that improve the fit and function of protective clothing. Include normal wear over the life of the item.

The cost of job search

You can deduct certain types of expenses related to job searches, if you're already working and looking for a different opportunity within your field. You can, for example:

- Travel expenses, lodging, and mileage related to interviews

- The fees paid by employment agencies to placement and search firms

- The cost of sending professional resumes

- Costs associated with job coaching, skills testing, and career counseling

- Pre-employment licensing, drug testing, and other requirements

- Accessing online job databases or attending virtual job fairs is charged.

It should not be to launch a career, but rather find employment within your existing field. If you're unemployed or entering a different field, your expenses will not be deductible.

Professional Development and Education

You may be eligible for a tax deduction if you spend money on additional education and training to improve your job skills or maintain them. Common examples include:

- The cost of tuition, books, supplies, equipment and registration fees

- Attending conferences, workshops, seminars and classes can cost you money in travel expenses and mileage.

- Subscriptions to professional journals, association dues and reference materials

- To retain certifications and credentials, you must pay licensing exam fees

- Review and tutorial courses for maintaining certification

Training and courses offered as part of a voluntary program to prepare you for advancement, or to launch a brand-new profession are not eligible. Professional education is deductible if the training was required by your employer or a widely-accepted minimum standard mandated for you to practice in your profession.

Maximizing Tax Deductions

Be sure to adhere to all rules when claiming these job-related expenses and maintain detailed documentation. Here are a few key tips.

- Keep a log of all business-related data, including mileage, phone calls and travel costs, home office time, dates, and times.

- Keep original receipts that list the date of purchase, total amount, type of item purchased, name and address for vendor, as well as payment method. To reduce the fading of paper receipts, scan or photograph them.

- Print out additional copies of the receipts to add to your credit card statements and bank statement.

- To simplify tracking of expenses, pay work-related costs from a different business account.

- To avoid missing any deductions, record them as soon as possible. Add up and total your records as early as possible in the tax season before you file.

- You can use the standard rate of mileage for your operating expenses instead. Business mileage rates are usually adjusted annually.

- Use tax preparation software or an accountant to determine the best deduction strategies and maximize write-offs.

Be on the lookout for red flags which can cause IRS to scrutinize excess deductions without proof of business purposes. To ensure compliance, consult a tax expert to avoid penalties or interest if the IRS challenges your claim.

If the W2 employee can prove their expenses, they may be able to reduce taxable earnings. It is important to keep track of costs throughout the year, and maintain thorough documentation in order to qualify for deductions.

Red Flags for Excessive Deductions in The IRS

Everyone wants to lower their annual taxable income by as many eligible deductions as they can. Claiming excessive or incorrect deductions may attract IRS attention, and trigger audits. These situations can arise even if you make a mistake due to unclear regulations.

Knowing the "red flags", which may cause the IRS to examine your tax return more closely, is helpful. Most issues can be avoided if you adhere to the deduction guidelines and provide solid substantiation.

The following are common triggers that increase IRS scrutiny:

1. **Taxes Deductions that are not proportionate to income**

A red flag can be when your total dollar amount or percentage seems to be disproportionately large compared to the income you have reported. Tax evasion and fraud may be suspected in low- to moderate-income filers who claim $30,000 worth of write offs. Auditors look at your entire return to see if there are any inconsistencies.

2. Dramatic Increases in Claiming Expenses

IRS systems will often flag for review any significant increase in total deductions from year to year without a good business reason. If you notice sudden increases, it's likely that something is wrong. Documentation must be provided to prove the major changes in your life. In general, deductions that increase in line with income growth are not questioned.

3. Industries and roles with known abuses

Due to past issues, those who run cash-oriented businesses such as restaurants, retail stores, personal service providers or sole proprietors are more likely to be scrutinized. W-2 employees can take advantage of positions that allow for mileage reimbursement, travel compensation or home office deductions. They may also purchase supplies and equipment. IRS monitors closely these groups to ensure they are legitimate compared with actual income.

4. The description is vague or missing details

IRS computer screens return for specifics about each category of deduction. The exact expenses must be listed for terms like "travel", "supplies", and "travel". Failure to do so could lead to audits requesting additional proof. If you fail to provide these details, penalties may be imposed or deductions could be rejected due to insufficient information.

5. Larger Round Numbers, Estimates Lacking Precision

Using round numbers, such as $15,000 in supplies or $20,000 for travel expenses to claim thousands of dollars suggests that you are estimating your costs rather than tracking them down to the penny. The majority of legitimate deductions are based on precise, jagged totals that reflect actual spending records and financial records. If you don't account for each dollar, it can be interpreted as exaggeration.

6. Delay in reporting previous years' expenses

IRS believes that most large purchases and expenditures will appear on tax returns during the year they were made. This is called "constructive receipt". Auditors suspect that you have fabricated or backdated your deductions when they appear on your return in 2022. Credit/debit matching will help you to prove that the timing is accurate.

7. Unusual purchases that lack business relevance

IRS examines the direct relationship between income and assets, equipment or other activities that are not part of a person's profession. If an Uber driver deducted a photo equipment, or if a CPA claimed extensive photography gear, the IRS would need to know why.

8. Doubtful Home Office Tax Deductions

It is still one of the areas where people abuse this deduction, despite having limited resources, a small space and clearly using it for personal purposes like watching television. The IRS will closely examine any potential overstatements, such as deducting the full cost of a home renovation or large utility bills to cover minor freelance work at night.

9. Claim 100% of Business Use

In the same way, cars, mobile phones, computers, and many other assets are used at least partially for personal use, resulting in a reduction of deductions after dividing them up. It is difficult to believe that an expensive item or category was used "100% for business purposes only". This requires more evidence. Broad claims invite audits.

10. Lavish Travels, Meals or Leisure Activities

Tax code allows deductions of ordinary and necessary business expenses. However, extravagant travel, such as expensive sports junkets or luxury European trips, requires taxpayers to prove that the primary goal was revenue production, not vacationing. Only 50% of entertainment and meal costs are deductible. Excessive claims will be subject to accountability checks.

11. Sloppy records and insufficient documents

Audits are often triggered by vague, cryptic records that lack comprehensive travel itinerary, receipts or any other tangible verification. IRS will then fill in all the gaps. Partially missing documents won't increase IRS scrutiny. However, large amounts of deductions without supporting documentation will prompt IRS correspondence.

12. Dodging Paper Trails, Cash Payments

IRS is suspicious when they see that cash was used to pay for large purchases. They also look at missing receipts and records, or credit/debit cards. Auditors will pay more attention to significant expenditures that are not accompanied by documentation or credit card trails.

13. Shared business and personal expenses

IRS is more likely to be concerned about the proper division of costs between nondeductible and deductible expenses when money, shared accounts and assets are used both for business and private purposes. Insufficient data to assign expenses into the correct categories and co-mingled activity can lead to inflated write-offs.

How to Protect Yourself from A Future IRS Audit

Anyone can feel stressed and intimidated by an IRS audit. The IRS audits are designed to confirm the validity of tax returns, deductions, payments and income. Even the most honest of taxpayers might be asked to provide additional documentation during intense questions.

Audits are rare, and affect less than 1 percent of all filers each year. Certain risk factors can increase the chances of an audit. Preventative measures can be taken to reduce IRS scrutiny, and you will also be prepared in the event of an IRS audit. These are some important tips to protect yourself.

Understanding Key Audit Triggers

IRS examines returns for mathematical irregularities and areas where taxpayers have abused the system in previous years. Audits can be triggered by dramatic increases in deductions, extravagant purchases without a business reason, the delaying of expense claims into future years and excessive expenses.

Understand which industries and occupations are more likely to be scrutinized, such as cash-only businesses. Annually review risk scenarios to prevent unintentional behaviors that trigger reviews.

Maintain Impeccable Records

Documentation is essential. Keep detailed mileage logs and travel itinerary, as well as receipts with all details, to support any deductions you claim each year. You are vulnerable to IRS inquiries if you don't have solid proof.

Confirm the figures carefully

Double check, before filing your return, that the income generated from these activities is equal to all business expenses deducted. If you are experiencing losses, it is important to be concerned unless temporary conditions exist. Ensure that the total of all deductions does not exceed your annual income. This will automatically trigger audits.

Provide Specifics Information

If your deductions are disproportionately large for your income and occupation, IRS will send you a letter requesting more details if the description is vague. Use tax preparation software to add details such as precise amounts, vendor names, location, and purpose. Avoid basic ambiguity.

Audit Defense Services

Hire firms that offer audit representation and defense services, including correspondence to appeals. Professionals can handle the procurement of documents, defend your position, negotiate with IRS agents directly, and accurately translate tax code terminology.

Correction of Innocent Errors

You should respond promptly to IRS notifications about mathematical discrepancies or unreported income. Also, you must provide missing forms and clarifications. Uncorrected errors can raise suspicions and lead to full audits. Do not let minor problems grow into larger ones.

Limiting Cash Transactions

Paying major vendors via electronic or check creates a paper trail that is impartial. IRS can suspect that you are hiding payments "under the tables" if you rely solely on cash without third-party verification. Report all income honestly and keep receipts as proof of deductions.

Don't take frivolous tax positions

IRS fines for underpayment of taxes linked to fraud can trigger an audit the next year. Do not take questionable positions like declaring your taxes as voluntary, or trying to say you are exempt from the filing and payment obligations because you are a "sovereign citizen". These frivolous actions will be subject to a thorough review.

Business & Personal Segmentation

To avoid mixing expenses, if you are a freelancer or run a side business, make sure to use a dedicated credit card, specialized checking account, and other assets for the enterprise. Separating financials from discrete tax entities can reduce the chance of misclassifications, and audit chances are lower because there is less ambiguity.

Chapter 8

Claiming Tax Credits and Benefits

Various credits and benefits are available under the federal tax code to assist taxpayers who may be in a particular situation, like raising children, attending college, purchasing a house, or having a modest income. The provisions are essentially subsidies that are administered by the tax code.

The chapter discusses the most important personal tax benefits and credits that taxpayers may be eligible for in order to lower their total tax obligation. These credits and deductions include:

- Earned income tax credit (EITC).

- Child Tax Credit

- Credit for Work Opportunity

- Lifetime Learning Credit

- Interest on mortgages

- Tax Credit for Contributions to Retirement Savings

It can be difficult to determine eligibility criteria and adhere to rules surrounding these provisions. This chapter is intended to provide key information on eligibility, calculation, claim, refund ability and other important topics. The reader will discover how to distinguish between credits and deductions. They'll also learn about phase-outs, what benefits are refundable, etc.

This knowledge will allow taxpayers to identify and claim new tax benefits and credits. It can result in substantial savings on taxes and hundreds of thousands of dollars more relief for people. This chapter enables readers to make the most of these subsidies.

What is a tax credit?

Tax credits are amounts of money which taxpayers may deduct directly from their tax liabilities. Tax deductions lower an individual's income, but this is not the same.

Tax credits are valued differently depending on their nature. Some tax credits can be granted to businesses or individuals in certain locations or classifications.

Understanding Tax Credits

The federal and state government may offer tax credits for specific behavior that benefits the economy, environment or any other important factor that they deem to be of importance.

A tax credit, for example, is offered to people who install solar panels at home. Some tax credits can be used to offset costs for child care and education.

Tax credits offer a better deal than tax deductions, as they reduce the tax burden dollar-for-dollar. A deduction reduces the tax bill, but only within an individual's marginal rate.

For example, a person in the 22% marginal tax bracket would be able to save $0.22 per dollar of marginal tax deducted. A credit, however, would lower the tax obligation by $1.

Types of Tax Credits

Tax credits are divided into three types:
- Nonrefundable
- Refundable

Nonrefundable Tax Credits

Tax credits that are not refundable are deducted directly from a taxpayer's liability for tax until it equals zero dollars. The taxpayer isn't given a refund if the amount owed exceeds the refund. The term nonrefundable refers to the part of the tax credit which cannot be used.

Tax credits that are nonrefundable are only valid for the tax year in which they were reported, are not carried forward to subsequent years, and can have a negative impact on low-income tax payers who are often unable use all of their credit.

Examples of tax credits that are not refundable include:

1. Adoption Credit

2. Lifetime Learning Credit

3. Residential energy credit

4. Credit for Work Opportunity

5. Credit for Child and Dependent care

6. Credit for dependents

7. Tax Credit for Contributions to Retirement Savings

8. Child Tax Credit

9. Credit for mortgage interest (helps taxpayers with lower incomes buy a house)

1. Adoption Credit

Adoption credit can help reduce the financial burden of legal adoptions. The maximum federal credit for adoptions is $14.890 per child in tax year 2022. The credit is available for all adoptions, including those that are agency, domestic, international, sibling groups, special needs and foster care.

Taxpayers with a modified adjusted gross (MAGI) below $223 410 are eligible for the full credit. The credit is gradually phased out for those with MAGI above $223,410. It will be completely gone once the MAGI reaches $263,000. If you maintain the proper documentation, all adoption costs, including agency fees, court costs, legal costs, travel costs, and costs associated with court proceedings, are included. The credit can refund up to $14,890 for each child if it exceeds the taxes due.

2. Lifetime Learning Credit

Lifetime Learning Credit allows taxpayers to claim up to $2000 per return for tuition, fees of enrollment and other expenses related higher education. Credit is available for undergraduate, graduate or professional degrees provided that the school has IRS approval. Students from the family of the taxpayer who are enrolled for at least one semester can be eligible, provided that they have not been claimed by anyone else as dependents.

In 2022, the income limits for married filers will be $80,000 and $160,000 respectively. Once the AGI thresholds of $90,000 for single filers or $180,000 for married filers are reached, eligibility is completely eliminated. This credit cannot be refunded, so it can only lower taxes to zero and not give a refund. The Lifetime Education Credit cannot be combined with other educational benefits such as tuition deductions in the same tax year.

3. Residential Energy Credit

Installing energy efficient equipment such as windows, doors and roofs with the Energy Star label can qualify homeowners for tax credits. Solar electric installations are eligible for 30% credits. Credits range from 10-30% on product purchases. No credit limits are set for life, but there are annual limitations per upgrade type implemented by Congress. Income levels do not affect eligibility. According to 2022 regulations, if the tax credit is greater than taxes due, only 500 dollars can be reimbursed.

4. Work Opportunity Credit

Work Opportunity Credits provide employers with incentives to hire individuals who represent groups that have consistently high rates of unemployment or employment barriers. These groups may include veterans, youth disconnected from the workforce, people referred to vocational rehabilitation, those who have been unemployed for a long time, SSI beneficiaries, or ex-felons.

The WOTC can reduce the federal tax burden of employers by thousands for each new employee who qualifies. Credits range from 25-40% depending on the target group and number of hours worked during the first year. There are extensive documentation requirements and certifications. Credits that do not exceed taxes due can be carried over for up to twenty years.

5. Child and Dependent Care Tax Credit

CDCC assists working taxpayers in paying expenses for care of a child or dependent under 13 years old or incapable of taking proper care themselves so they can continue to work or actively search for employment. The CDCC covers expenses for daycare, preschool, and day camps (not overnight camp).

Taxpayers can deduct up to 35 percent of the costs of up $3,000 for a single child/dependent, or $6,000 for multiple children, resulting in a maximum of $1,000 or $2,000. The claimed expenses are reduced by the pre-tax benefits for dependent care that have already been claimed. For those earning less than $15,000, the full credit of 35% is available. The percentage slowly drops to 20% up to $43,000.

6. Credit for dependents

Other Dependents credit provides a $500 tax credit to certain dependents who do not qualify for the $2,000 Child Tax Credit. The Other Dependents Credit provides a $500 tax credit for certain dependents who do not qualify to receive the $2,000 child tax credit. A taxpayer who claims a dependent must provide more than half of their annual needs.

This $500 tax credit is not income-based. This credit allows high-income earners who have older children with dependents or relatives that are dependent to get a similar tax break to the child's tax credit. This credit, like regular tax credits reduces tax liabilities and doesn't refund excess amounts.

7. Tax Credit for Contributions to Retirement Savings

This credit is also known as the Saver's Credit. It provides a tax credit that's non-refundable based on a certain percentage of contributions made by taxpayers to retirement plans like 401(k), 403(b), SIMPLE IRAs, SEPs, and conventional IRAs.

In 2022, the maximum credit for 50% is $1000 for single filers or $2,000 for married couples filing jointly. For married couples to qualify for the maximum 50% credit they must have an AGI below $41,000 and contribute up $4,000 (for single filers, it is only $2000). On a sliding scale, partial credits can be granted up to $68,000 AGI per couple and $34,000 for singles. The higher income earners receive credits of 20-10% before the phase out is complete.

8. Child Tax Credit

Child Tax Credit (CTC) is an American tax credit that's available to taxpayers who have children younger than 17 years old at the end of each year. The credit for 2023 (the return filed in 2024) is $2,000 per qualifying child.

If you are an individual taxpayer, your income must not exceed $200,000 or $400,000. Joint filers can earn $400,000. Parents with high incomes will see the benefit diminish over time.

Child Tax Credit reduces the total tax owed by taxpayers on a dollar-for-dollar basis. This is better than tax deductions, which lower total income and result in less savings.

Many people who have low incomes don't file taxes, because they are aware that they do not owe money. This can be wrong for a number of reasons.

Tax returns are mandatory for all but those with the lowest earnings. You may also be missing valuable benefits. If you are a parent, the child tax credit is partially refundable if combined with the additional child tax credit. You can get a portion of the credit back, even if your taxes are not due.

A taxpayer who wants to claim the Child Tax Credit must submit Form 1040. Individual Income Tax return. A taxpayer is also required to attach Schedule 8812, entitled "Credits for Children and Dependents Qualifying".

Credits are available for dependent children who meet certain criteria:

- Has not yet reached the age of 17 by the end the year.

- Are you a stepchild, foster or adopted child, sister/brother/stepsister, half-brother/half-sister (or descendant) of one of these family members?

- You have lived with him for at least half of the year

- Contributed less than half his/her own support

- A dependent has been claimed on your tax return

- If you have not filed jointly with your spouse or if the only reason for filing is to get a refund on estimated taxes paid

- Are you a U.S. national or citizen?

9. Mortgage Interest Credit

Mortgage Interest Credit is a tax credit that helps taxpayers with lower incomes who earn below certain thresholds to pay for mortgage interest. It involves complex rules around types of eligible mortgages and residences along with exact income cutoffs based on tax filing status - ranging roughly $50,000-$67,500 single/$100,000-$135,000 married filing jointly.

The eligibility test is a simple two-test system that confirms income under annual limits and also spends a percentage or more of income on mortgage interest. The credit amounts are 10% to 50% after deducting the allowable amount used for primary standard/itemized deductions. The credit, which is less well-known, was created to help eligible homeowners with lower incomes.

Refundable Tax Credits

The most advantageous tax credit is a refundable one, because it's paid in full. The taxpayer is entitled to receive the full amount, regardless of income or tax liabilities. If, by way of example, the refundable credit lowers the tax due to $0 or less, the taxpayer will be entitled to a specific refund.

The Earned income tax credit (EITC) is one of the most common refundable credits. EITCs are available to low- and moderate-income earners who work for an employer, or as self-employed individuals and can meet specific criteria regarding income and family size.

It is also refundable. The credit helps families and individuals pay for the premiums of health insurance through the marketplace.

Some tax credits only offer partial refunds. The American Opportunity Tax Credit for students in postsecondary schools is one example.

The remainder of the tax credit can be used as a refund credit, up to the lower of either 40% or $1,000.

As a result, of the Tax Cuts and Jobs Act, it became refundable up to $1500 in 2022 and as much as $1600 in 2023.

Earned Income Tax Credit

Earned income tax credit is among the most generous and beneficial credits for lower-income workers in America. The tax amount owed is reduced and you may receive a refund. EITC amounts vary based on your income, marital situation, and the number of children you have. For the tax year 2022:

- For taxpayers without children, the maximum EITC is $560. Income limits for qualifying range between $7,320 and $16,480. For married couples filing jointly, the income limit is $7,320-$22,610.

- The maximum amount of the credit is $3,733. The income limits for single filers range between $10,640 and $43,492, while for couples, the limit is $10,640-$49,622.

- The maximum income increases to $6,164 for two children and $6,935 with three or four. Income ceilings rise accordingly.

- Joint filers also face a higher phase-out of credit than individual taxpayers.

For EITC eligibility, you must satisfy the requirements for earned income, investment earnings, filing status and employment status.

Basic Qualification Rules

You must meet the following requirements to qualify for EITC:

- You have worked but earned income below $63,398

- If you have a total investment income of less than $11,000 for the year 2023

- By the deadline for your return in 2023 (including any extensions), you must have a valid Social Security Number.

- You can be a U.S. resident or citizen all year.

- Do not file Form 2555 Foreign Earned income

- If you're separated from your partner and are not filing joint returns, there are certain rules to follow.

Rules for Special Qualification

There are special rules that apply to the EITC.

- Members of the Military

- Clergy members

- The Taxpayer and Their Relatives with Disabilities

Valid Social Security number

For you to qualify for EITC benefits, each claimant on your tax return must possess a valid Social Security Number (SSN). The SSN has to be:

- Valid for Employment

- If you want to extend the deadline for filing your tax return, please make sure that the extension is issued **in advance of** this date.

We accept the Social Security Number on the Social Security Card that says "Valid to work with DHS Authorization."

We don't accept the following for EITC:

- ITINs are the individual taxpayer identification numbers

- Adoption of taxpayer identification number (ATIN).

- Social Security Numbers on Social Security Cards that say "Not valid for employment"

Status of Filing

You can qualify for EITC by using one of these statuses.

- Married filing jointly

- Head of the household

- The surviving spouse is eligible for the benefits

- One-Sided

- Separate filing for married couples

If you have a child that qualifies and has lived with you more than 50% of the year you can apply for the EIC.

- If you lived separately from your spouse during the final six months of the year or

- If you are separated legally according to the state laws, either by a separation agreement in writing or a separate maintenance decree and did not live with your spouse after 2023.

Use our EITC Qualifying Assistant or Interactive Tax Assistant if you are unsure of your status.

Heads of Household

If you are not married, and you pay for more than half of the cost of maintaining your house where you reside with your child who qualifies, you can claim Head of the Household status.

Qualification of Surviving Spouse

All of the following must be true for you to qualify as a widow or widower:

- You **may have** prepared a joint tax return for your deceased spouse. No matter whether you have filed a joint tax return.

- You claim the EITC if your spouse passed away less than two years prior to the year for which you are claiming it .You did not marry before the year's end.

- More than half of the annual cost to maintain a house was paid by you

- If you have a stepchild or child, then that is a claimable relative. Foster children are not included.

- The child was in your house all year except for a few short absences. **Note:** A child born during the year or a child that died in the same period is not eligible for this exemption.

Maintaining a House

You can meet this requirement if you have paid at least half of the costs to maintain a house during the year in which you filed your tax return.

Included in the cost are:

- Rent, mortgages, property taxes, and insurance

- Repairs and utilities

- Home-cooked food

- Public assistance pays for some costs

Costs don't include:

- You can use money you received from the Temporary Aid for Needy families or any other government assistance program.

- Clothes, vacations and education expenses

- Prescription drugs, health insurance and medical treatment

- Insurance for life

- Transport costs such as insurance, leasing payments or public transport

- Renting out your home

- The value of the services you provide or of those provided by a household member

U.S. Citizen or Resident Alien

If you are filing jointly, both your spouse and yourself must be U.S. Citizens or Resident Aliens to claim the EITC.

You or your partner can claim EITC only if you are married and filing jointly, and you were or you spouse was a resident alien during any portion of the year.

- U.S. Citizen with valid Social Security Number

- A resident alien in the U.S. for at least six months during the calendar year that you are filing, and with a valid Social Security Number

How to Claim EITC without a Qualifying child

If you meet these rules, then you can claim the EITC even if there is no qualifying child. If you are filing a joint return with your spouse, then both of you must meet the following requirements.

- Eligibility for the EITC is based on basic rules

- You must have your primary residence in the United States of America for at least half of the tax year.

    - It includes all 50 US states as well as the District of Columbia, and U.S. Military bases. The United States does not include U.S. territories such as Guam or the Virgin Islands.

- You cannot be listed as an eligible child on someone else's return

- You must be at least 25 years old but not older than 65 years (at least 1 spouse must fit the rule).

As soon as You will receive your refund

If the taxpayers chose direct deposit, and their returns are in order, they can expect to see most EITC/Additional CTC refunds on their debit card or bank account by March 1. Some taxpayers will receive their refunds earlier.

Additional Credits That You Might Qualify for

You may be eligible for additional tax credits if you are entitled to the EITC.

- Credit for Dependent Children and Other Dependents

- Credit for Child and Dependent care

- Educational Credits

Chapter 9

Organizing Key Documents for W-2 Tax Filing

We are getting closer to the end of the book. It's time to collect the paperwork. Your tax return will be easier to complete if you have all of your paperwork in the right order. If you have incorrect or missing information on important forms such as your W-2s, 1099s, and other tax documents, it could cause delays in filing your return.

If you report incorrect information, it may affect your refund amount or the amount that is owed. It is now critical to collect documents in order to meet the tax deadline. You can use the last few weeks to get any forms that are missing and check what you already have before filing your taxes. Implement consistent recordkeeping throughout the year in order to avoid last tax season's scramble.

Which documents do I need to file my taxes?

Check out the checklist for tax preparation below before you begin. Remember, if your partner and you are married, they will also need the information below.

Personal Information

The IRS and the state's taxing authority will use your personal information to determine who is filing a tax return, how they can contact you, and where their refunds are deposited.

The exact name that appears exactly on your Social Security card

- Date of Birth
- Number of Social Security
- Address
- Tax returns for the previous year, both federal and state

Direct deposit refunds require a bank account number, routing number, and your direct deposit number.

Dependent Information
You'll need to provide the following details if you want to claim another person as your dependent:

Date of birth and Social Security number (or Tax ID number) for dependents.

If the custodial parents of your child are relinquishing their right to claim the child as a dependent, then you should use Form 8332.

Document Needed

Collect other documents, like:

1. **1095-A Health Insurance Marketplace Statement**

The Affordable Care Act requires that people who purchased health insurance in 2021 through federal or state marketplaces collect Form 1095A. The marketplace will send you this form, which shows the months of coverage and the advance premium tax credit based on your income estimate. This form provides the information needed to reconcile actual premium tax credit eligibility with what was claimed.

Verify the correct details of the policy, including monthly premium costs and any advance credits applied. Before filing your taxes, report any differences to the marketplace provider. This form should be kept with your other tax documents so that you can enter the data into your tax software or give it to a professional tax preparer. Accounting for health insurance and credit affects taxes due or refunds.

2. 1095-B and 1095-C Statements of Health Insurance

Some taxpayers may receive two additional statements of health insurance: 1095B and 1095C. Insurance companies send Form 1095-B to confirm coverage months for insured policyholders and dependents. Self-insured employers must submit Form 1095 C detailing the months covered by employees and dependents.

Keep Forms 1095B and 1095C with your tax records to prove the minimum coverage required by the Affordable Care Act. These forms are handy to verify coverage if there is a question during the preparation of your return or an IRS inquiry. These forms may also be used to document eligibility for some tax payers who qualify for a health insurance credit if certain criteria are met.

3. Childcare Statements

For the purpose of filing factual information, people who pay for child and dependent care related to their work in 2021 are advised to retain any associated documents. Taxpayers who pay for qualified child or dependent care expenses may be eligible to receive tax credits, such as the Earned Income Tax Credit and the Child and Dependent Care Credit. Taxpayers must provide documentation to prove that they have paid for qualified expenses in order to receive these significant credits.

Ask for an annual statement showing the total costs per child in the prior tax year. Total all costs from different providers and programs that allow you or your spouse to work in 2021. Daycare costs, after-and-before school programs, preschools, day camps, and babysitters in your home are all eligible. You must also record the names, addresses, tax IDs, or social security numbers of recipients because childcare tax laws require it.

4. Student Loan Interest Statements

Documentation of student loan interest paid are allows for a possible deduction. By the end of the year, lenders send borrowers IRS Forms 1098-E detailing the student loan interest they paid in the previous year. The form includes the total amount of interest and any other information, such as origination fees that are treated as interest.

Before filing your taxes, check the accuracy of the 1098E form based on payments estimated to be made in 2021. The IRS allows taxpayers to deduct student loan interest up to $2,500 per year on their federal returns and, in some cases, state returns. The claim is easy to make if you have the right paperwork that proves interest.

5. Form 1098: Mortgage Interest Taxes

For homeowners who pay mortgage interest or real estate tax in 2021, documentation is necessary to reduce their potential tax liabilities. Mortgage lenders will send Form 1098 by January's end, detailing the mortgage interest and taxes that were paid. The form includes the mortgage interest, real estate taxes, and mortgage insurance, as well as points towards loan origination.

You can deduct up to 10,000 dollars of qualifying real estate and mortgage taxes by using Form 1098. To avoid IRS inquiries, verify that the information you provide reflects what was actually paid in 2021. Collect separate statements that show any points you paid for a home refinance or if you purchased a new loan.

6. Donations to Charities

Taxpayers who intend to deduct their contributions must provide proper documentation for each donation. Records acceptable include bank statements, statements of credit cards, cancelled checks, or letters from organizations. If you are claiming a deduction of more than $250, the charity must provide a written confirmation that shows the amount and date received.

It takes time to track down the donation records for last year, but it is important in order to prove deductions. To reduce the time spent on tax preparation, begin collecting contribution statements now and verifying large gifts. Use a tracking app to keep track of your charitable donations throughout the entire year. This will reduce the amount of paperwork while ensuring that nothing is missed and maximizing deductions.

7. Contributions to Retirement Plans

The year-end statement is required by taxpayers who are saving for retirement through 401(k), IRAs, or Roth accounts to show any possible tax deductions. By May 31, financial institutions that administer retirement accounts must issue IRS Form 5498, which shows annual contributions. The IRS Form 5498 is a statement that documents your tax-advantaged savings. It includes traditional IRAs, Roth IRAs, and HSAs, as well as any conversions or rollovers.

Before filing your taxes, review Form 5498 to ensure that you have an accurate record of all retirement contributions. Check that the estimated tax credits or deductions match up with your savings amounts. The IRA contribution cap for 2021 is $6,000 across traditional and Roth accounts. The catch-up contribution for people over 50 years old is $1,000.

8. Investment Income Statements

To accurately calculate tax, taxpayers who earn extra income in 2021 from their investments will need to have all the associated documents. Financial institutions will send out 1099s containing the total amount of dividends and interest paid by investment accounts to holders for the tax year prior on February 15, 2019. The year-end statement also shows any capital gains or losses from the sale of investment assets.

Gather all 1099-consolidated statements, along with any supplemental documents of stock sales that show the original cost and net proceeds. The documents will allow you to accurately calculate capital losses and gains that impact the taxation of your investment income. Documentation is key to obtaining the best tax rate for long-term gains.

9. Records of Side Income

Taxpayers may receive an additional 1099 forms, 1099 NEC, or 1099 MISC if they have performed other work and earned miscellaneous income. income. The 1099-MISC form is used to report income from sources like freelance work, consultancy, honoraria, commissions, or rents. IRs 1099-NEC, meanwhile, report compensation paid to non-employees such as independent contractors and self-employed people.

IRS regulations require that you look for 1099s from other income sources when gathering your tax documents. Sometimes, statements are sent to outdated addresses, causing problems for those who need these documents at tax filing time. Contact any companies you worked for as an independent contractor to ask them to resend the 1099 or to verify that no payments have exceeded IRS reporting thresholds. Documentation is essential to ensure accurate self-employment and income tax liabilities.

10. Estimating Tax Payments

Documentation is required for both self-employed tax payers and W-2 workers who make estimated tax payments throughout the year. Self-employed taxpayers must detail quarterly estimates of payments for Social Security, Medicare, and income taxes not covered by payroll withholding. Documentation is also required for W-2 employees who pay a quarterly estimated tax to cover any shortfalls that may occur outside of withholding.

Find cancelled checks, bank statements, or confirmation notices that show the exact estimated federal, state, and local tax payments that were made between January 1, 2021, and December 31st. Verify the amounts in order to receive proper credit for payments and possible refunds for overpayments. Receipts of every estimated tax payment will protect filers in the event that any are overlooked by tax authorities or incorrectly applied.

11. Loss Proof

Different types of losses are deductible. Documentation of these losses is required if you are affected.

Keep records of any investments or stocks that have lost all value or for which you plan to file a claim, such as the date and price at purchase.

Keep records of all non-business debts that are uncollectible. An example is when you loan money from your own bank to a friend and they do not repay the debt. It may take a while to gather all the information you require before filing your tax return, but you will have what you need to be able to claim any and every credit or deduction available.

If you are audited, keeping your tax records in a secure place can be very helpful. When the IRS examines your tax return, it may ask you to provide records that support the tax credits and income on your return. This will help you speed up the tax process and ensure that your credits or deductions are not lost.

Tax Filing Mistakes

Are you aware of the common mistakes made in tax preparation? You don't need to make a mistake when it comes time for tax season. Internal Revenue Service checks for errors and can impose harsh penalties. Avoid the common mistakes and oversights when preparing your tax return.

Avoid these mistakes

1. The basics are blown

Verify that you and your dependents' names are correctly spelled and the Social Security number is correct. Select the right filing status based on your circumstances. You can file for single status if you are unmarried. However, if you qualify as a widow or head of household with dependent children, you will be eligible for more advantageous tax rates. In certain circumstances, married couples can pay less overall tax if they choose to file jointly rather than separately. IRS.gov's Interactive Tax Assistant can assist you in choosing the right filing status. This is especially true if there are multiple options.

2. You don't enter information as it has been reported to you (and the IRS)

You can enter your wages, dividends and bank interest as well as other sources of income that you have earned. Enter the information carefully. The IRS has also received these forms, so the computers of the government are searching for the same information. Contact the company that paid you (for example, your employer), and ask for a corrected Form W-2. You can contact the IRS by calling (800) 829-1040 if you haven't received a corrected Form W-2 before the end of the month.

3. The items are not entered on the correct lines

Be sure to enter your information in the correct place on your tax form. Don't, for example, put the tax-free IRA transfer on the line that is meant to be taxable IRA withdrawals. Tax software can help you avoid this problem, but make sure to double check the final form before submitting it.

4. Standard deductions are automatically taken

You could end up losing money if you automatically take the standard deduction. While it is more difficult to itemize and requires receipts or other evidence, the automatic standard deduction can save time. You can check which option gives you a greater deduction. The standard deduction has nearly doubled since 2018 as a result of the Tax Cuts and Jobs Act. This means that itemizing will save you less money. The majority of tax software will automatically determine which method you are most likely to benefit from.

5. You don't take write-offs that you're entitled to

Many people may be afraid that certain deductions are audit red-flags and avoid them. Some people still believe, for instance, that taking a deduction for a home-office can lead to a tax audit. It's unlikely that this is true. The IRS has created an alternative deduction to write off the actual costs, and many people now work from home. It's a good idea to claim a tax deduction as long as it meets the requirements of your state or federal law.

But--and it's a major however--you may only deduct if your home office is used because you are self-employed. As a general rule, employees of businesses cannot deduct home office costs that are not reimbursed as an itemized deduction.

6. You forgot your state healthcare individual mandate

In 2019, The Affordable Care (ACA) Individual mandate was abolished. This mandate required that you pay a fee each month you (or members of your family) did not have qualifying health coverage. However, some states have their own individual health insurance mandate, so be sure you know what your state requires.

Six states, plus the District of Columbia and six other states have mandated individual health insurance as of 2023.

- New Jersey

- California

- District of Columbia

- Rhode Island

- Massachusetts

- Vermont (does not have a penalty for failure to comply)

7. You don't check for typos

Transposing a number is easy. You can also leave out one digit, which will distort your information. Say you made a $5,200 contribution to an IRA, but accidentally entered $2,500 on your tax return. This would cost you $648 in additional taxes if your tax bracket is 24%.

8. Math mistakes are common

Math errors can range from simple addition and subtraction to more complex calculations. These can be simple additions and subtractions or more complicated calculations.8 Double-check all your math or, better yet, use tax preparation software to do the math.

Check the IRS guidelines if you need to enter a number as negative. Other forms use a minus sign, while some prefer parentheses. The IRS computer will read your negative entry properly. If you wish to report a $500 loss on your tax return, then enter the amount as ($500), not (-$500).

9. You don't tell the IRS how to handle your refund

Be proactive when it comes to what the government should do with your refund if you have overpaid taxes. The U.S. Treasury Department will mail you a check if you do nothing.

To receive your refund faster, you can add the information about your bank (account and routing numbers) to ensure that it is deposited into your account. You can also choose to divide your refund among up to three different accounts. It can be used to pay for estimated taxes next year, to contribute to retirement accounts, such as IRAs, or to purchase U.S. Treasury Marketable Securities (e.g. Series I Savings Bonds). Your options are explained in the instructions to Form 8888.

10. Making payment errors

Make sure your tax payment has been correctly credited. Include Form 1040V in your check, whether you are filing on paper or electronically. You can also pay using the IRS approved payment providers or through one of the free government payment sites, such as EFTPS.gov and DirectPay. You can amend your U.S. return if you made a mistake using the Form 1040X Amended U.S. Individual Income Tax return

IRS Free File

The IRS Free File Program is an IRS-industry partnership that allows many companies to offer their tax filing and preparation software for free. The IRS Free File Program offers two free ways to file federal income taxes online.

- **Tax Guide** offers free online preparation of tax returns and the filing thereof at IRS partner sites. For those taxpayers who qualify, their partners offer this service free of charge. The IRS offers a free tax return to taxpayers with an AGI of $73,000 or less.

- **Fillable Free Forms** is an electronic version of federal tax forms. It's equivalent to the paper form 1040. If you need to, use IRS publications and form instructions to help prepare your tax return. This option is free for taxpayers with an AGI greater than $73,0.

What Is the Eligibility for Free Files?

The threshold for 2023 was $73,000 in income or less. Income thresholds apply to all filing statuses. The limit is based on your adjusted gross income, not your gross income.

Some providers have extra requirements, such as income or age restrictions. The IRS reports that in 2023, over 20 state filings will be available.

How Does the IRS Free File Program Work?

Free files can be accessed through the IRS site. Free files are not advertised on some providers' websites.

There are two ways to access Free File: you can either browse each service provider or use the IRS online search tool. You will be asked a few questions regarding your tax credit eligibility, filing status, and adjusted gross income. It will then run the answers you provide through the system in order to determine which free file program is best for you.

What you need to get started

Personal Information

- You will need to have a copy of your last tax return (for the previous year) in order to get your adjusted gross income (AGI).

- You, your spouse, and your dependents, as applicable, must have valid Social Security numbers.

Revenue and receipts

- Benefits of Social Security

- Unemployment Benefits

- You may need to keep receipts for your business.

- Rent, royalty, partnership, S-corporation, trusts, income receipts

Additional Income

- Your W-2s show all your wages for the year.

- 1099-INT: Form showing the interest you received throughout the year

- The Form 1099G shows any state or local tax refunds, credits, offsets, and/or credits.

- The Forms 1099-DIV and 1099-R show dividends or distributions paid from your retirement plans and other plans during the calendar year.

ACA filers

- Health Insurance Marketplace Form 1095A. Affordable Care Act (ACA) tax provisions provide more information.

- Form 8962, Premium Tax Credit

Electronically File

- You must validate and sign your electronic tax returns when you self-prepare your taxes. Use your AGI from last year or the self-selected personal identification number that you used to verify your identity. Use a 5-digit PIN (as long as it does not contain all zeros) to sign your tax return electronically.

- Sign in to your account if you don't know the AGI from last year but have your tax return from that year. It is the easiest and fastest way to access and view your previous year's adjusted gross income.

- You can request a transcript of your tax return by post if you cannot access your account online.

Contact information

- To receive a notification from Free File Software that the IRS has accepted your tax return, you must have a working email address.

Benefits of the Free File Program

- **A free federal return is available.** As a new Free File user, you may choose the Free File offer of a company based on their offer qualification criteria listed at IRS.gov. You will not have to pay for the preparation of your federal tax return or e-filing if you qualify.

- You will get an email welcoming you to the official IRS Free File service from your previous company if you have used IRS Free File in the past. Emails must contain a link that takes you to the IRS Free File website of the company and provide instructions on how to use it. You will not have to pay for e-filing a federal return if you select this link.

- **There are no fees to file a federal return.** Participants in the Free File Program do not charge any fee to file a federal tax return. Free File participants will never ask you to purchase any product or service (such as promotional rebates) in return for preparing your federal tax return.

- The IRS Free File does not include bank products that charge fees. You must not receive bank products with fees as part of the IRS Free File.

- **Free state returns may be available.** Some IRS Free File Program partners offer free state tax preparation. Some charge an additional state tax. Make sure you read the information that each company provides.

- **Every Free File Company guarantees the accuracy of return calculations.** This guarantee is listed on each company's website. If you have any concerns about accuracy, contact the company that prepared your return.

- **There are options:** In the event that you do not qualify for an IRS Free File after visiting the Free File company website, you may return to IRS.gov Free File to search for a Free File offering that meets your requirements. If you do not qualify for an IRS Free File offer, each IRS Free File provider will give you the information you need and provide a link to IRS.gov Free File.

- **Get help when needed. If** you have a problem while you're on the IRS Free File website of a business and you're doing your tax return, please contact their free customer support.

- IRS Free Files offers an online search tool to help you locate the offer that best suits your needs.

Other Tax-filling provider

If you are not eligible to use the IRS free-fill program, here are other tax-filling providers, including:

Provider	Other requirements for qualification
1040Now	• AGI: $65,000 or less. • There are no age restrictions. • All states except AK, FL, NH, NV, TX, WA, and TX. • State returns are not free, but they can be purchased for an additional $17.95.
TaxReturn: ezTax	• AGI: $73,000 or less. • There are no age restrictions. • AL, AR, AZ, CA, CO, GA, IL, LA, MA, MD, MI, MO, MS, NC, NH, NJ, NY, OH, PA, SC, VA, WA, WI • There is no free state return. However, it can be purchased for $19.95.
FileYourTaxes.com	• AGI: $3000 to $73,000 • Age: 66 or younger. • All states are eligible for a free federal tax return. • IA, ID, ND, and VT state returns are free. States that do not receive support can add $50.
FreeTaxUSA	• AGI: $46,000 or less. If on active

Provider	Other requirements for qualification
	duty, $73,000 is the limit.
	• There is no age limit.
	• All states are eligible for a free federal tax return.
	• All states are eligible for free state tax returns. State returns are $14.99 if you do not qualify for the free federal offer.
Online Taxes (OLT)	• AGI: From $11,100 up to $73,000
	• There is no age limit.
	• All states are eligible for a free federal tax return.
	• All states are eligible for a free state tax return.
TaxAct	• AGI: less than $73,000 Some states may allow people 67 years of age and older to qualify. For more information, visit the IRS Free File Website.
	• Aged 20–64 years.
	• All states are eligible for a free federal tax return.
	• AR, IA. ID. MS. MT. ND. RI. VT. WA. WV. State returns are $39.99 for states that do not have support.
TaxSlayer	• AGI: $73,000 or less. This offer may be available to you if your income does not meet the guidelines, but

Provider	Other requirements for qualification
	you are still eligible for EITC.
	• Age: 58 or younger.
	• All states are eligible for a free federal tax return.
	• AR, AZ, DC, GA, IA, ID, IN, KY, MA, MI, MN, MO, MS, MT, NC, ND, NY, OR, RI, SC, VA, VT, WV. State returns are $39.95 for states that do not receive support.

Chapter 10

Effectively Communicating with Your Accountant

In this final chapter on tax preparation for W-2 income earners, this chapter addresses best practices for communicating with a tax professional or accountant. Even if all your income comes from one source (i.e., employer-provided W2), strong interactions between tax professionals can save you money during tax season.

We will provide tips for selecting a trustworthy tax preparer, providing all pertinent documents from this year, and asking smart questions regarding deductions or credits you might qualify for. Proactive communication and organized preparation can maximize your tax preparation service experience and optimize any refunds you are eligible to claim.

Here are a few guidelines designed to make tax preparation an efficient yet financially beneficial process.

Selecting a Reputable Tax Preparer

Selecting an accurate tax preparer is key to making sure that your taxes are done accurately and that you take full advantage of every deduction and credit available to you. Even with income coming only from W-2 employers, investing in professional preparation can reap considerable savings. Here are some important guidelines for selecting someone reliable:

Qualifications to search for

When selecting the qualifications of a tax preparer, be sure to focus on their experience, specifically in personal income taxes. Preferably, look for one with one or more of these qualifications:

Certified Public Accountant (CPA): CPAs have passed rigorous licensing exams and satisfied extensive educational and experience requirements, making them experts in complex tax situations, but even for straightforward W-2 filers who file taxes themselves, working with one may prove advantageous due to their knowledge of tax codes and filings.

Enrolled Agent (EA): EAs are licensed tax specialists by the IRS who have passed an extensive taxation exam covering every facet of personal taxation, audit, and appeal procedures and represent clients before the IRS for audits or appeals proceedings, much like CPAs possess expertise that goes far beyond typical software solutions or chain preparers.

Accredited Tax Preparer (ATP) or Accredited Tax Advisor (ATA): These credentials from the Accreditation Council for Accountancy and Taxation require candidates with prior experience preparing taxes to pass one or both exams before taking an ATP or ATA examination, representing training specific to personal tax return preparation.

State-Certified Tax Preparer: Some states administer their own licensing programs for tax preparers who operate within them, and state-certified preparers meet legal standards of knowledge and education on taxes in those jurisdictions.

Any one of these credentials—CPA, EA, ATP/ATA certification, and state certification—indicates extensive training and expertise from tax preparers who can efficiently address your situation.

Explain Your Tax Situation

As part of selecting and hiring a tax preparer, it is vitally important that you provide information regarding your personal history and situation up front. Even if your only income consists of W-2 income without deductions, providing this background helps the preparer understand your needs better. Share details, such as:

Income Sources: Outline your employment situation, such as how long it has been at its current place or any changes. Furthermore, list any sources of additional income, like interest payments, dividends, or retirement fund withdrawals, and discuss those of any spouse as well.

Have you prepared your taxes yourself, at chain stores, or with an individual CPA or enrolled agent? - Involving our audience in previous tax preparation experiences helps establish context and create meaningful dialogue.

Major Life Events: Discuss any major life changes that might impact taxes in the near future, such as marrying, divorcing, separating, having children, adopting new children, buying property, leasing property, changing jobs or careers, retiring, paying college costs, or unexpected income events like inheritance, lottery winnings, a new business venture, or major moves that could impact taxes.

Prior Audits or Issues: Be sure to inform the tax preparer if any previous tax returns or amendments due to errors have been audited, amended, penalties assessed, or taxes due; discuss penalties or tax debts too so as to prevent surprises on audit. Being open about all aspects of your tax history and situation—both past and future plans that could impact it—allows a preparer to gain an accurate assessment of how best to prepare, deduct, or plan your return based on life changes, tax credits you qualify for, or plan ahead for taxes in general. Be honest when sharing this information to establish long-term, trusting tax advisor relationships. Share all necessary details right from the beginning!

Understanding your accountant's language

If you can't communicate with your accountant, you will waste your time and effort. Accounting terminology and acronyms can be difficult to translate. Learn their language and seek clarifications when necessary. Here are a few terms you may hear from your accountant:

Don't be alarmed if the language your accountant speaks sounds foreign. It's easier than you think to understand your accountant. You're familiar with concepts like the DOR, leveraged investment, or your P&L.

These acronyms and phrases will become familiar to you as time goes on.

1. P&L

P&L, or profit and loss statement, is another name for the income statement. The financial statement summarizes all of your income and expenditures for a specific time frame (month, quarter, or year).

The P&L report shows that we have exceeded our budgeted operating income for the quarter but are still on target to reach our sales targets.

2. Gross Vs. Net

The terms gross and net are used to describe income. However, they can also be applied to anything else that is countable. *The net* is the sum after any deductions. *Gross is* the amount before reductions.

For example, "Gross revenue is looking great this month, but after subtracting product returns, our revenues have been weaker than what we would like to see."

3. Accruals

Accruals can be income or expenses that are due over time. Accrued insurance costs are common because you can get the same protection throughout the entire year even though you only pay twice a year. You can accrue your insurance by recording one-sixth each month. Then, when paying your bill biannually, you will adjust any difference between the accrued and actual amounts.

Even though we won't receive payment from the client until the next quarter, the revenues were accrued when construction began.

4. Leveraged

Accounting terms like "leveraging" refer to a company taking out a loan in order to purchase an asset. It's not necessarily good or bad to leverage investments, but the majority of companies will only do so when they can outweigh their borrowing costs with investment revenues. When it is cost-beneficial.

Ex: "The cost is high." To make an appealing offer, we'll have to use our credit line.

5. Capital Account

When discussing an investor's investment, the term "capital" is commonly used. For example, the capital account of an S corporation share holder will start out at the original price paid by the shareholder for the stock and be adjusted each year for the portion they receive from the net profit. Capital accounts may also be adjusted to reflect other factors, including assuming liability, taking a shareholder's loan, adding additional capital, or making distributions.

For example, "When last year I borrowed money from a shareholder, my capital fell, and my distribution this year may be subject to tax."

6. Disclosure

Disclosures are additional details that accompany and provide a detailed description of the financial statements. Disclosures are used by entities to clarify numbers and highlight important details. GAAP-compliant entities have to follow specific rules. The narratives often explain the figures in the income statement, balance sheet, cash flow statement, and shareholder equity statement. However, many of these disclosures also include graphs or figures.

For example, "The new disclosures for revenue recognition may require time to perfect. Let's start working on them as soon as we can."

7. The DOR

The acronym for the Department of Revenue is DOR. The acronyms for other state and federal government agencies, such as the Department of Commerce (DOC) and the Department of Labor (DOL), are also similar.

For example: "We called the DOR in your name and asked why you got that notification."

8. POA

The Power of Attorney (POA) is a state-specific document that allows a third person to act for another. Powers of attorney (POAs) are state-specific documents that authorize a third party to act on behalf of another.

For example, "Once the POA is signed, we can contact the Secretary of States' office to determine how the ruling on tax will impact the tax return."

9. Amount

Accounting apportionment can be used to divide revenues and costs into groups. The most common use of this term is state tax apportionment. This is where the net income of a company is divided up and apportioned among the various states that they are operating in. For state taxes, apportionment is calculated by combining sales, payroll, and property data.

Example: Since we lost the North Carolina distribution channel, I anticipate that our North Carolina allocation factor will go down this year and my Georgia apportionment factors will increase.

You can clearly see that the accounting language is a dialect of the business language with some slight differences. You and your accountant can discuss the health of your business more effectively when you understand these accounting terms.

The Right Questions to Ask

Asking questions is another way to be proactive. Asking the right questions can help you discover a new opportunity that you would like to pursue, or a weakness you could easily fix.

W-2 income earners likely qualify for more tax deductions than they realize, potentially yielding substantial annual savings. Navigating all the IRS rules alone is no simple task - having an experienced tax preparer provide invaluable services by asking key questions to identify deductions tailored specifically for you while making sure documentation is handled accurately. Some good questions include:

1. Deductions Related to W-2 Income

Although your tax deductions for W-2 income will likely be smaller than they would be as an independent business owner, some key ones you could claim include:

Home-Related Expenses: As a homeowner, you could potentially deduct mortgage interest, property taxes and certain insurance costs as deductible items; plus certain home office expenses if telecommuting part time (based on IRS guidelines). A tax professional will help determine your deductible amounts based on this.

Donations to Charity: Any contributions you make to eligible non-profits with IRS approval qualify as charitable deductions; there may be rules regarding limits and documentation needs, however.

Medical Expenses: Any healthcare-related expenses exceeding 7.5% of your adjusted gross income for the year can be deducted, including insurance premiums, doctor/dentist/vision visits, prescriptions and mileage costs related to appointments; fertility treatments or long-term care expenses may also qualify as deductions.

Child and Dependent Expenses: Your expenses associated with caring for children or dependents in your household could potentially qualify as tax deductible deductions, including childcare expenses while working, school costs and tuition payments - such as preschool costs in some instances.

Contributions to Retirement Accounts: Any contributions that you make during the tax year to an IRA, 401(k), HSA, or similar retirement plans could qualify as tax-deductible expenses.

State/Local Taxes: Deductions may also apply for state income taxes paid, vehicle registration fees or local income taxes paid.

2. Eligibility Rules

IRS regulations detail eligibility rules for every deduction type. They specify expenses count towards qualifying deductions and qualifying and claiming amounts; age criteria; income phase outs; and more complex parameters that make keeping track of them difficult as an individual taxpayer.

Utilizing your preparer's knowledge of current eligibility guidelines is invaluable when trying to maximize write-offs legally. A qualified preparer should ask specific questions regarding your family, home, health expenses, charitable giving contributions, and retirement contributions in order to assess where deductions may apply and ask targeted follow-up questions accordingly.

Your tax preparer may inquire into these key details:

Home offices qualify for deductions by providing square footage used, home size, utilities and internet costs as well as date placed into service. When it comes to medical expense deductions - your income, exact cost incurred as well as insurance reimbursements all should be reported accurately for deduction purposes.

3. Which Records Are Needed

As with charitable deductions, receipts showing total donations per group as well as their type (cash, property or volunteering), are necessary. With childcare deductions such as costs incurred while working and provider tax ID numbers as well as number and income level details being relevant are needed for claims purposes. C. What Records Need to be Maintained for Deduction Purposes?

Not only can tax preparers identify deductions you qualify for, but they can also advise what paperwork must accompany these amounts as per IRS regulations. Accumulating receipts, statements, and appraisal records to support deductions is imperative to passing audit scrutiny if ever audited.

Your preparer can offer guidance regarding required proof, such as:

Charitable Donations - Please provide the following documents when making charitable donations of $500 or greater: 501(c)(3) confirmation letter, bank/credit card statement displaying amount due, valuation documentation.

Medical Expenses: Provide proof of medical expenses via invoices from care providers, explanations of benefit forms from insurers, and pharmacy printouts documenting prescription costs. Home Office: The homeowner should present evidence that proves total home square footage, including bills related to utilities, internet, and insurance allocated specifically to the office space, as well as photos showing where everything will take place within that office space.

Property Taxes: Statement from your tax collector's office showing amounts due and paid, plus invoices detailing payments; mes Retirement Contributions: Year-end statements from 401(k) and IRA plans showing contribution amounts

4. When to Inquire

Timing is everything when considering potential deductions; with tax year-end quickly approaching, decisions may still be made to expand some write-offs legally. Your tax preparer can advise on end-of-year moves related to:

Charity Giving: Donations must be in by December 31st, so inquiries should begin in mid-December. Non-cash gifts valued over $5,000 require a qualified appraisal by qualified appraisers; please allow time.

Medical Expenses - If your medical expenses fall just within the 7.5% deduction threshold, January prepayments could help get over that hurdle more easily. Consult your tax preparer by early December about this option as early payments could potentially help save on tax fees and save time with deductions.

Job Expenses: Unreimbursed costs such as training, travel, or equipment can qualify if they exceed 2% of income. Have these details ready by mid-January so your preparer can complete paperwork on them.

Conclusion

Taxes as a W2 worker may appear straightforward, but it takes planning and preparation to truly understand your situation. We have seen in this book that even though W2 employees receive their tax and income payments deducted already, many other factors can impact your tax return and any refunds or additional taxes you may owe.

We discussed in the first chapter the importance of aligning financial goals with tax planning. It is difficult to balance building long-term wealth with minimizing taxes. Tax-advantaged savings and retirement accounts are available for W2 employees. They can be powerful tools for lowering taxable income while saving money. Tax deductions on traditional IRAs as well as pre-tax contributions to 401Ks or FSAs allow you to pay taxes at a later date when you are in a lower tax bracket.

Next, we discussed what types of income are taxable as well as the different tax rates. The income you earn from wages, interest, and dividends is fully taxed. However, certain incomes, such as scholarships, military allowances, and gift assets, are eligible for preferential tax treatment. The total tax paid by a W2 worker is composed of federal, state, and Medicare, as well as Social Security.

This statement lists all applicable taxes and income for the entire year. Each line on the W2 form was examined in detail, from gross wage to Social Security, Medicare, withheld federal and state taxes, as well as retirement contributions and dependent care. It is important to double-check all the details of your W2 before you file your taxes.

A summary of how to prepare for the tax season includes best practices such as gathering documents, forms, and statements. Organizing tax documents and tracking them on an online platform or tax preparation software can make it easier to stay on top of everything needed for a complete and accurate filing.

All taxpayers have to choose between itemized or standard deductions. The higher the standard deduction, the better the tax reduction. The key itemized expenses related to homeownership, charity donations, medical costs, state and local taxes, as well as the current limits on deductions and qualification for tax deductibility, were discussed in depth.

We have outlined the significant short- and long-term tax advantages these accounts offer by letting contributions grow tax-deferred. We outlined the significant short- and long-term tax advantages these accounts offer by letting contributions grow tax-deferred. Set Max Contribution retirement contribution limits help steer your planning and budgeting for these tax minimization approaches.

Taxes are unpleasant, but getting money back in tax benefits and credits makes it easier. Tax credits for education, family, home ownership, retirement savings, and child or dependent care are all common tax credits that can reduce or increase the amount of your refund.

We also discussed the best ways to communicate with your accountant or tax professional in order to ensure accurate filing of returns. By organizing the forms and supporting documentation, you can better understand your tax situation. This includes income sources, eligibility for deductions, life changes, etc. Understanding taxes is a continuous process for W2 employees. This book should help you establish good financial planning, filing, and tax obligations.

Thank you for reading and kindly leave a review. Please check out our website at BOOKPASSION.NET where we're constantly posting content focusing on improving quality of life, one book at a time ☐

Appendix A

Glossary of Tax Terms

A

- **Adjusted Gross Income (AGI):** Your income after accounting for certain deductions is used to calculate your taxable income.

- **Allowance:** A set amount of money an employer withholds from your paycheck for income tax purposes.

- **Amortization:** the process of spreading the cost of an intangible asset (e.g., goodwill) over its useful life.

- **Audit:** An IRS review of your tax return to verify its accuracy.

- **The American Opportunity Tax Credit (AOTC)** is a credit for qualified education expenses paid for an eligible student for the first four years of higher education. You can get a maximum annual credit of $2,500 per eligible student.

B

- **Basis:** The original cost of an asset used to determine capital gain or loss when it is sold.

- **Business Expense**: An ordinary and necessary expense incurred in your job or running a business that can be deducted from your income.

C

- **Claimant**: The individual who files a tax return.

- **Credit:** reductions in your tax bill that you can claim based on certain circumstances. Common credits include the earned income tax credit, the child tax credit, and the education credit.

- **Capital Gains:** The profit you make when you sell an asset, such as a stock or a piece of property, for more than you paid for it. Capital gains are subject to taxes.

- **Capital Losses:** The loss you incur when you sell an asset for less than you paid for it. Capital losses can be used to offset capital gains, which can reduce your tax liability.

D

- **Deduction:** an expense or allowable expense that reduces your taxable income.

- **Dependant Care Credit**: A tax credit for expenses incurred for childcare or care for dependent elderly or disabled individuals.

- **Dependent:** A person who qualifies for you to claim a tax deduction on your return.

- **Depreciation**: it is the decrease in the value of an asset over time due to wear and tear or obsolescence.

E

- **Exemption:** A deduction that reduces the amount of income subject to tax.

- **Earned Income Credit (EIC)**: A refundable tax credit for low- and moderate-income earners.

- **Estimated Tax Payments:** Quarterly payments made throughout the year to avoid penalties if you expect to owe more than $1,000 in taxes when you file your return.

F

- **Filing Status:** Your marital status and dependents determine your filing status (e.g., single, married filing jointly, head of household).

- **Form 1040:** it is the main federal income tax return form that most taxpayers file.

- **Federal Income Tax Withholding:** The amount of federal income tax that your employer withholds from your paycheck each pay period. The amount of withholding is based on your Form W-4, which you give to your employer.

- **Federal Income Tax:** A tax that you pay to the federal government on your income. The amount of tax you owe

G

- **Gross Income:** Your total income from all sources before any deductions or adjustments.

H

- **Home Office Deduction:** A deduction for expenses related to a dedicated home office used for business purposes.

- **Hourly Wage:** The amount of money you are paid for each hour you work.

I

- **Individual Retirement Account (IRA):** A type of retirement savings account with tax advantages designed to encourage future financial security.

- **Itemized Deductions**: A list of specific expenses that you can subtract from your AGI to reduce your taxable income. Common itemized deductions include medical expenses, state and local taxes, and charitable contributions.

J

- **Joint Return**: A tax return that a married couple files jointly.

M

- **Marginal Tax Rate:** The tax rate applied to each additional dollar of taxable income.

- **Medical Expense Deduction:** A deduction for qualified medical expenses exceeding 7.5% of your AGI.

- **Mortgage Interest Deduction**: A deduction for the interest paid on a mortgage for your primary residence.

N

- **Non-Taxable Income**: Income that is not subject to income tax, such as gifts, inheritance, and certain types of benefits.

O

- **Ordinary and Necessary Expense:** An expense that is common and accepted in your line of work and is incurred to produce income.

- **Overtime:** Any time you work beyond your regular scheduled hours. Overtime pay is usually one-and-a-half times your regular hourly wage.

P

- **Payroll Taxes:** Taxes withheld from your paycheck for Social Security, Medicare, and federal income tax.

- **Penalty:** A fine imposed by the IRS for failing to meet tax filing or payment deadlines.

- **Personal Exemption**: A deduction of a standard amount for each taxpayer and dependent. (No longer in effect as of 2023)

- **Pre-Tax Dollars**: Money deducted from your paycheck before taxes are applied.

R

- **Refund:** The amount of money the IRS sends you if you overpaid your taxes.

- **Roth IRA**: A type of IRA where contributions are not tax-deductible but qualified withdrawals in retirement are tax-free.

S

- **Standard Deduction:** A fixed amount of money that you can subtract from your AGI, even if you don't have any itemized deductions. The standard deduction amount varies depending on your filing status.

- **State Income Tax**: A tax levied by your state on your income.

- **Social Security Tax:** A tax that you pay to help fund Social Security, a government program that provides retirement benefits to eligible workers. The Social Security tax rate is 6.2% of your wages.

- **State Income Tax Withholding:** The amount of state income tax that your employer withholds from your paycheck each pay period. The amount of withholding is based on your state's tax laws.

T

- **Taxable Income:** Your income remaining after subtracting all allowable deductions and exemptions.

- **Tax bracket:** the range of income that is subject to a certain tax rate. The U.S. federal income tax has seven tax brackets, ranging from 10% to 37%.

- **Tax Audit:** A review of your tax return by the IRS to verify that you have reported your income and deductions accurately.

- **Tax Penalty:** A fee that you may have to pay if you don't file your tax return on time, pay your taxes on time, or meet other tax obligations.

- **Tax Lien:** A legal claim that the IRS can place on your property if you don't pay your taxes

- **Tax Refund:** A payment that you receive from the IRS if you have overpaid your taxes.

- **A traditional IRA** is an individual retirement account that allows you to save for retirement with tax-deferred benefits. Contributions may be tax-deductible, and earnings grow tax-deferred until withdrawn in retirement.

U

- **Unearned Income:** Income received from sources other than your job, such as interest.

V

- **Vehicle Mileage Deduction:** A deduction for business miles driven in your own vehicle.

- **Voluntary Payment:** An optional payment made with your tax return to contribute to specific government programs.

W

- **Wages**: Your taxable income earned from employment.

- **Withholding:** The amount of taxes your employer deducts from your paycheck and sends to the IRS.

- **W-2 Form:** A form your employer sends you each year that shows how much you earned and how much tax was withheld from your paycheck.

- **W-2 Employee:** A W-2 employee is a person who holds a formal position of employment with a business or organization in the US and who receives a W-2 tax form each year to report their income and taxes withheld.

Y

Your Federal Tax Form: The specific form you need to file your federal income tax return (e.g., 1040, 1040-EZ).

Additional Terms:

401(K) Plan: A retirement savings plan is offered by some employers that allows you to contribute a portion of your paycheck before taxes are taken out.

403(b) Plan: The 403(b) plan is an account for retirement that's available to those who are employed in the public sector

457 Plan: It is a type of tax-advantaged retirement savings account that certain state and local governments and tax-exempt organizations offer employees.

Appendix B

State-Specific Tax Information

Below, you'll find links to each state's tax forms. Find your state's site to download the necessary forms and get started filing your state income tax.

Alabama	Kentucky	North Dakota
Alaska	Louisiana	Ohio
Arizona	Maine	Oklahoma
Arkansas	Maryland	Oregon
California	Massachusetts	Pennsylvania
Colorado	Michigan	Rhode Island
Connecticut	Minnesota	South Carolina
Delaware	Mississippi	South Dakota
District of Columbia	Missouri	Tennessee
Florida	Montana	Texas
Georgia	Nebraska	Utah
Hawaii	Nevada	Vermont
Idaho	New Hampshire	Virginia
Illinois	New Jersey	Washington
Indiana	New Mexico	West Virginia
Iowa	New York	Wisconsin
Kansas	North Carolina	Wyoming

Table of figure

www.ingramcontent.com/pod-product-compliance
Lightning Source LLC
Chambersburg PA
CBHW060013210326

41520CB00009B/867